A Stage Manager's Survival Guide

From Callbacks to Closing

Michelle Marko

Copyright 2015

A Stage Manager's Survival Guide: From Callbacks to Closing

Contents

Opening Note
1. Key Characters
    - Tip 1: Check your ego at the door.
    - Tip 2: Walk a mile.
    - Tip 3: R-E-S-P-E-C-T!
2. Qualifications: What It Takes To Kick Ass
    - Tip 4: It's all your fault, so own it!
    - Tip 5: It's a small world.
    - Tip 6: Embrace the chaos.
    - Tip 7: Let your passion shine.
3. Auditions/Callbacks
    - Tip 8: Listen to all. Share what's necessary.
    - Tip 9: Start off on the right foot.
4. Production Meetings
    - Tip 10: Take obsessively detailed notes.
    - Tip 11: Clarity with schedules.
    - Tip 12: Don't panic!
5. The First Rehearsal
    - Tip 13: It begins before the beginning.
    - Tip 14: Establish ground rules.
    - Tip 15: Your number must be their best friend.
6. The Rest of Rehearsals
    - Tip 16: Laugh. Breathe. Take more notes.
    - Tip 17: Be consistent.
    - Tip 18: "Thank you."
    - Tip 19: The drama ends with YOU!
    - Tip 20: Stick it to them by taking the professional high road.
    - Tip 21: You are your reputation.

A Stage Manager's Survival Guide: From Callbacks to Closing

7. Tech Week
   - Tip 22: Paper tech will keep you sane.
   - Tip 23: Be prepared. Then prepare some more.
   - Tip 24: Pad the time table!
   - Tip 25: Everything changes.
   - Tip 26: You set the mood.
   - Tip 27: Know when to follow the plan and when to go with the flow.
   - Tip 28: Take care of your crew.
8. Opening
   - Tip 29: SLEEP!
   - Tip 30: Double checking.
   - Tip 31: Stay calm. You got this!
   - Tip 32: Have fun, but not hangover fun.
9. The Run
   - Tip 33: Keep it fresh and consistent.
   - Tip 34: Have fun!
   - Tip 35: Don't get comfy.
10. Closing
    - Tip 36: Acknowledge the work everyone did.
    - Tip 37: Enjoy not being in charge!
    - Tip 38: Rest and reward.
    - Tip 39: Even the worst show closes, and makes the best stories.
    - Tip 40: There is always something new to learn.

A Stage Manager's Survival Guide: From Callbacks to Closing

Opening Note

This book is meant to offer tips and tricks to new stage managers as they navigate the chaotic world of theatre, and to compliment more formal training or detailed manuals. While there are plenty of ways to do all the things a stage manager does, hopefully these survival tips can help you to experience more of the exhilarating moments, and learn to laugh at the stressful ones.

By: Michelle Marko, copyright 2015

A Stage Manager's Survival Guide: From Callbacks to Closing

Chapter 1: Key Characters

It takes an army of people to run a theatre and put on a production. Everyone from the people who answer calls about tickets, to designers solving impossibly quick costume changes, to actors creating an experience the audience will feel and not just watch. All of the roles are important, and all are needed for a show to be great. As the stage manager, you'll likely be working or interacting with almost all of them.

SURVIVAL TIP #1: Check your ego at the door.
The official hierarchy might vary from theatre to theatre. However, I personally think the more important thing to consider is the relational hierarchy. My first few shows out of college, I thought the stage manager was the boss and proceeded to take that to an obnoxious extreme. Telling the director we had to end rehearsal at a certain time because parents were there to pick up their kids, never mind the director only wanted 5 more minutes to finish the scene and the parents would have loved to watch a little of the rehearsal. Another time I decided that the schedule said actors had to be off book, so that meant no scripts in hand and proceeded to scold the cast accordingly. I immediately paid the price for that one since I had a massive amount of line notes to write. A power trip, I learned, was the fastest way to start off on the wrong foot and alienate the very people I wanted to build a relationship with. While the stage manager might be in charge, the truth is that they need to partner with people, not boss them around. The partnership also changes since the relationship to the stage manager alters depending on what phase the show is in. Below is a visual of the most productive setup that I've come across, however it can vary per theatre.

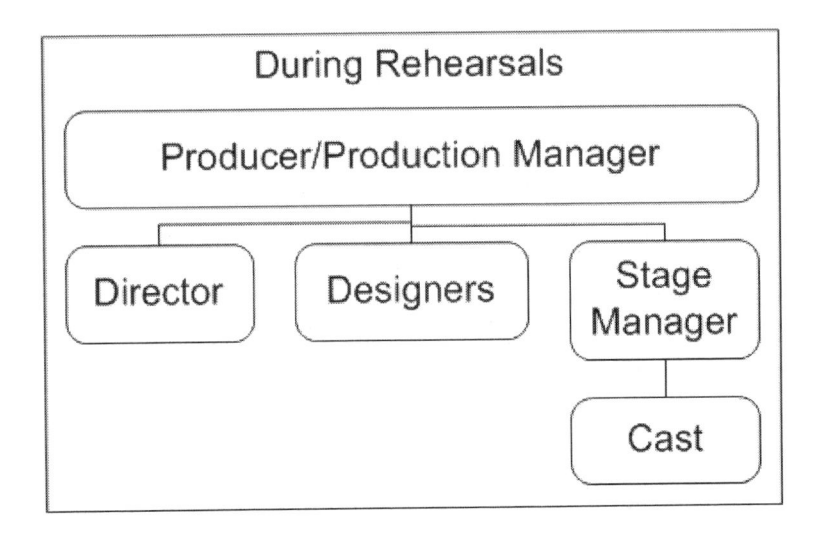

A Stage Manager's Survival Guide: From Callbacks to Closing

During Rehearsals

Producer/Production Manager
- Director
- Designers
- Stage Manager
  - Cast

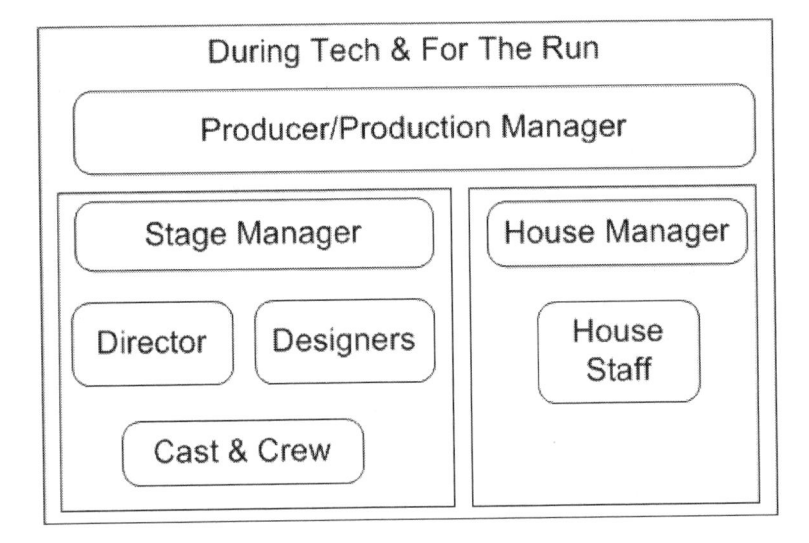

During Tech & For The Run

Producer/Production Manager

- Stage Manager
  - Director
  - Designers
  - Cast & Crew
- House Manager
  - House Staff

Traditionally, directors have "turned over the show" to the stage manager on the first day of tech. However, this is not an excuse for a power

A Stage Manager's Survival Guide: From Callbacks to Closing

trip, which is why I don't show a direct line. The director doesn't "report to you", but is someone you need to respectfully manage.

The Who's Who of the What's What

Directors: The person with the vision of the show. The relationship between a stage manager and a director can make or break a production. It is critical for a stage manager to understand how the director works, and be willing to adjust to their style. Do they plan every detail in advance? Has the blocking been thought out months ago? Or do they prefer to walk through the show and feel how the movement should go? As a stage manager, you have to do your best to be open to both styles. For the director that feels their way through things, try to keep them on schedule and keep an eye on the bigger picture - as long as things are going forward, all is well. For the director who plans everything out far in advance, do your best to keep up with their schedule and accept that it's ok for you to let go of some control on scheduling.

I've been fortunate to work with directors with diverse styles, and in the process also came to understand which styles allowed me to thrive as a stage manager, and which ones made me want to run for the hills. In general, I love a director who has the blocking planned out, the schedule planned out, and is generally very organized. However, one of my all-time favorite directors to work with is much more free-flowing. She is a favorite because we just "get each other" and are able to complement each other's strengths. I keep her on schedule, and she is extremely patient with me when I get stressed out. In time, you'll learn who your favorites are. Be sure to cultivate those relationships, and continue to do as many shows as you can with them. When working with a director that has you questioning your reason for being in theatre at all, just remember that all shows must close. Take note of what tactics you used to try and improve things, and how they helped or made things more intense. Essentially, stop to recognize how this experience will help you spot a director you can work well with in the future. And next time that person asks you to stage manage, be sure to have a few suggestions of fellow

By: Michelle Marko, copyright 2015

A Stage Manager's Survival Guide: From Callbacks to Closing

stage managers who might have a better matching personality to offer with your polite and professional "no thank you" response.

Designers: These are the folks with a specific creative vision for their field. Typically, a show will include designers for: lighting, sound, set, costumes, and props. Depending on the production, you might also have wig designers, special effects designers or fight choreographers. In an ideal world, their vision of the show is in-line with the director's vision. This is most likely to occur when the two parties have had countless phone calls and chats about the production and what they're trying to accomplish. In a worst case scenario, these conversations will only happen at production meetings. If that is the case, make sure you add an extra hour to the meeting time allotted as these discussions are critical to creating a beautiful show. Also keep in mind that while you are likely only working on one show at a time, designers are often working on multiple shows at multiple theatres simultaneously. Keep this in mind when scheduling with them, and also be sure to list the theatre and show in the subject of any email. Sending them an urgent email with "Costume fittings needed now!" when they have two shows going into tech and only one is yours is a great way to cause unnecessary stress and panic.

House Managers/Staff: You likely won't see much of the house manager until the show is running, but when you do see them, go introduce yourself! They will be your partner in crime during the run of the show. It is important to coordinate the house opening, curtain, and intermission end with them for each performance. If something goes wrong with your dimmer check, it is the house manager who has to face the potentially frustrated audience and tell them what's going on. By having them focus on the audience, you are free to focus on the cast, crew and show itself. Never underestimate the value they bring to the production. I've worked with fantastic House Managers and extremely clueless ones over the years. Let me tell you, a disorganized stressed out house manager can cause delays, aggravate patrons and throw off your routine for the night. Avoid this by communicating with them, learning their

A Stage Manager's Survival Guide: From Callbacks to Closing

style and asking how you and the crew can help. Keep in mind what you and the crew should help with will vary from theatre to theatre; the important thing is that the house manager knows you've got their back if they need it.

Being appreciative and respectful also goes for any of the concessions staff or ushers. For most theatres, these folks will be volunteers. Keep this in mind and make sure you represent the theatre well at all times. Be polite. Say "please" and "thank you" if you have them help you with something. However, don't be afraid to be assertive. I've had a few concession volunteers think it was ok to wander around backstage in the green room before a show. Upon seeing them standing there, I asked how I could help and then escorted them out. Often times they will wander backstage looking for me, on behalf of the house manager. On the few times where they "just wanted to see what it was like", I politely explained why we don't allow non-essential people back there before a performance. This policy will vary from theatre to theatre. If it's ok for staff to wander around, the more the merrier! As long as it doesn't interfere with the performance and any pre-show activity.

Production Manager: Not all theatres have a production manager, but for the ones that do, oh my you want them to be your best friend! This is the person that will find your crew, deal with contracts, and often help with scheduling production meetings. They are the poor soul stuck dealing with all the practical details of staffing a production. Be sure to let them know your crew needs early on so they have time to find the best people possible. Also, be sure to tell them your schedule as it relates to the season, so they know which shows you are available for. As with everyone, be sure to show your appreciation for what they do. As a role that often functions in the background, it is easy for them to be taken for granted. DON'T EVER TAKE THEM FOR GRANTED. Over the course of my career, I've seen the difference of having or not having a production manager can make! When there is a production manager, it has made my stage management life so much easier and more productive. As such, I do my best to constantly say thank you, express my appreciation, and generally ask what I can do to make their job easier. The result? I've had the crew I needed for every

A Stage Manager's Survival Guide: From Callbacks to Closing

show; I don't have to worry about who has signed what, and production meetings just happen! It's magic I tell you!

Crew: These are the various backstage people you manage from tech to closing. It is important to remember that for most theatres and productions, the crew joins the production later in the process, so be sure to make them feel welcomed! I have found time and time again that regardless of how intense and complex the technical needs of the show are, if I have a happy crew, then I have a happy show! While we are all there to enjoy the process of producing a show, with large crews it is equally important to make sure they stay on task and understand what is expected of them from the start. Set aside time to meet with just the crew at the first tech rehearsal to talk through what you need from them and what they can expect from you. Remember to thank them after every rehearsal. Chances are the harder they work, the less you'll notice them, so don't forget to show your appreciation to them just as you do with the cast. I have found that if I take care of my crew, they take care of me. As many of my lightboard and sound ops can attest to, I am notorious for calling the "stand-by-go" cue (when standby and go are all said at once because I forgot to give the standby earlier). Since I provide my crew with the tools they need to succeed (scripts, shift sheets, etc.), I know that we'll still have a great show even if my cue calling is occasionally a bit chaotic.

    It is also vital that the crew understands exactly how they are contributing to the show's success, as well as knowing that we are all a team. Make sure actors understand how the crew contributes and encourage crew and cast to mingle and get to know each other. Depending on the theatre, there might be separate areas for people to spend their free time, but if they are sharing a common green room it is critical that there isn't any "them vs. us" nonsense. While there might be individual personality conflicts, as there are with any group of people, I have found that having a zero tolerance policy for "them vs. us" prevents unnecessary stress during the run. No one needs a dresser who refuses to help with a change, or an actor who exits the wrong side to avoid a run crew person they simply don't want to see. Yes, both of those have happened to me. The costume change, I had a few dressers on hand

A Stage Manager's Survival Guide: From Callbacks to Closing

for the show and since the nature of the conflict was personal, I was able to re-assign the dresser. For the actor and run crew, I had a talk with them and had to mediate the discussion because there was no other option but for them to get along. In the end they agreed to be professional, and were. In my mind, my crew is as valuable and critical to the show's success as the cast. I do my best to show them this through my actions, and in my experience, it works. You'll see how over time all of the things you do to make the crew feel appreciated and welcome will pay off, as you won't have to look hard or go far to find however many crew you need for future shows. Assuming they don't graduate and move to New York or Australia.

Actors/Singers: These are those amazing people who bare their all, though usually just metaphorically, to the audience each and every performance. They are typically very passionate about their craft and will spend far more hours than you will see working on the show. Never take that for granted. Just as a stage manager spends many hours outside of rehearsal and performance working on the show, so do the actors. You should do everything in your power to support their efforts and encourage their success, just as you do with the crew. Sometimes their artistic temperaments can be a bit intense, but remember, everyone in theatre has some sort of artistic temperament. They put up with yours just as you put up with theirs. In the end, it is key that the cast know you appreciate and value their contributions to the show, and be sure they understand and value what others have contributed as well. You are not their parent though. You are their stage manager. Foster that relationship as theatre is a small community. Chances are high that you will work with many of the same actors, especially if you remain in the same market.

It is also important to remember they spend much of their time in a show staring at bright lights that are hotter than the sun. When they ask for glow tape and fans, do what you can to help them. Not all actors have the crew's ability to see in the dark and never sweat.

A Stage Manager's Survival Guide: From Callbacks to Closing

SURVIVAL TIP #2: Walk a mile.

Since those first few years out of college, I've had the pleasure of working on over 60 productions at eight theatres. I've been able to work in almost every technical role; except costumer designer, a role that remains a glorious mystery to me. Having walked a mile in the shoes of a set designer, prop master, actor, technical director, etc. made me a well-rounded stage manager. It gave me a keen insight into the needs and struggles of each, which has been invaluable in problem solving over the years.

If you don't have the opportunity to actually do various crew positions or design a show, not to worry! It's still possible to understand what is critical for each designer to succeed. How? Ask them. Go grab coffee with a lighting designer you respect, a costumer you regard highly, a director, a prop master, a wig master, a make-up artist, a few actors, and especially a technical director and production manager. If you are sincere in your interest, people are more than willing to share their world with you. Whenever possible, I highly recommend assistant stage managing or being on run crew for a new-to-you theatre. This allows you to observe how that specific theatre operates, as no two are the same, and to learn some tips and tricks from another, hopefully more experienced, stage manager.

SURVIVAL TIP #3: R-E-S-P-E-C-T!

Everyone from the people who answer calls about tickets, to designers solving impossibly quick costume changes, to actors creating an experience the audience will feel and not just watch deserve to be treated with respect. Everyone's contribution is important, and all are needed for a show to be great. Aretha Franklin said it perfectly; it's all about respect, as in treating people with respect and appreciation at every step of the way. This includes the concession volunteer who is convinced you are in charge of toilet paper, the actor who needs to take a break during tech even though everyone else doesn't need one, or the run crew who think that sweeping the stage is beneath them. In each of these situations, it is important for the stage manager to take a breath and respond professionally and in a way you would want to be responded to.

A Stage Manager's Survival Guide: From Callbacks to Closing

Venting might be required at a later time to keep your mind from exploding, but never in front of anyone involved with the show. If you treat everyone with respect, you'll find that the "diva moments" will decrease and you'll gain a reputation for being professional and exceptional to work with.

A Stage Manager's Survival Guide: From Callbacks to Closing

Chapter 2:

Qualifications: What it takes to kick ass.

Over the years I have learned that a job posting for a stage manager should really read "Wanted! Someone who is slightly nuts, has a great sense of humor, is open minded, flexible and has a healthy obsession with office supplies." Yes there are other important qualities such as organization, peace-keeping skills, problem solving, patience and the ability to lead and follow. But when you get down to it, the stage managers who come out of a production with a smile on their face, and aren't the ones curled up in the corner after strike still shaking and pleading "just make it stop", those ones – the great ones, are a little nuts, obsessed about putting lists everywhere possible, open minded to bizarre solutions, flexible (because nothing ever goes "on schedule"), and have more variations of sticky notes, pens, and Band-Aids than anyone ever should.

If that doesn't scare you, and even excites you, eliciting a "HELL YES" response, you have the heart of a stage manager and likely already have a few great stories to share. If the above terrifies you to the bones, don't fret, we were all sane and thought the above was nuts at some point. After you have a few tech weeks under your belt, and keep these survival tips in mind, you'll get there too.

SURVIVAL TIP #4: It's all your fault, so own it!

Everything that happens in a performance is the stage manager's responsibility. The wrong line spoken, the prop that doesn't make it on stage, the prop that gets left on stage, the lights that blackout too soon, the costume that falls off unexpectedly; it's up to the stage manager to make sure none of this happens. However, the beauty and excitement of live theatre is that it is never the same show twice and you never know what will happen. A great

A Stage Manager's Survival Guide: From Callbacks to Closing

stage manager does all they can to prevent errors, but when things go wrong, that great stage manager owns it. Take your lumps, accept the responsibility and focus on finding a way to make sure it doesn't ever happen again. Perhaps another item on a checklist, some extra safety pins backstage, or a note in your script that the light cue is a quick blackout. Whatever the issue, there is ALWAYS a solution. It's your job to find it and focus on making sure the next performance is smoother than the last. If you're stuck on a particular issue, brainstorm with your assistants, tech director, production manager or other stage managers as is appropriate. Often times a fresh set of eyes can help you find that magical way to do a complicated set change in only two shifts. Just because it's your responsibility, doesn't mean you have to solve everything alone. Theatre is a team effort. Be brave enough to leverage that team.

One such time for me was with a holiday show I worked on that was made of several one-acts. Each scene was a complete and total set change. I created beautiful shift sheets with the director's original plan which had a lovely flow of clearing out the old to then establish the new. On paper it looked great. In practice it took twice as long for every set change as anyone wanted. Ultimately, we found a different solution for each transition that was efficient and still lovely. And I do mean "we". The final shift sheet was a result of input from the director, the crew, the actors, the set designer, and myself.

On the flip side, when everything goes right, it's because of the talented actors, crew, designer and director. Do not expect accolades and everyone to say "it all went smoothly because of our amazing stage manager." While I have heard that after more than a few shows, it is always a welcome and appreciated surprise, but not an expectation. Remember that you are a stage manager, you don't get a spotlight or a bow during curtain call. In all the Tony speeches I've ever heard or read, never once do they say "thank you to my amazing stage manager." However I'm sure they deeply appreciate everything that stage manager did for them. Don't let this get you down though, because when you have a cast that shows their appreciation openly, it will warm you to the heart and help carry you through the next tough project. Keep every card and note of gratitude given, when I'm working hard with a

A Stage Manager's Survival Guide: From Callbacks to Closing

group that doesn't know how to say thank you, reading those notes from past shows helps put a smile back on my face and remind me why I continue to work in theatre.

SURVIVAL TIP #5: It's a small world.

While we live in a great big world, always remember that the theatre world is remarkably small, and oh boy, do we all talk! Not everyone gets along, but that's no excuse for being unprofessional. I've had plenty of folks I didn't quite click with, and those who I drove crazy. However, we found ways to be professional and work together. For a stage manager, I've found your reputation is as important, if not more important, than your resume. In fact, I've only had two formal interviews. Every other theatre I've worked with was due to my reputation, not a piece of paper.

One of the many joys of theatre is that we're a close-knit community. So that actor you tortured on that last show and told off in a glorious loud fashion? Yea, they likely talked to the director about you, maybe the artistic director and a producer or two. That next show at the theatre you've been waiting your whole life to stage manage? Nope. Not going to happen because the producer talked to the director from the other show.

There are two sides to this coin. While above all else, you should always keep things professional, it is equally important for you as the stage manager to share observations with the directors and producers as appropriate. An actor who was disrespectful to you or the cast, is an important thing to share. A lighting designer who went on a tirade about the lack of sufficient lighting equipment is not as important to share as everyone is likely already aware of this issue. The male crew member who creeped out the female cast members by staying in the green room that doubled as the dressing room, while they were stripping down and getting into costume at the top of the show; very important to resolve the issue immediately and inform the artistic director as it could turn into something much more serious.

There's no extensive list of what should be shared and what should be forgotten. Use your judgment, and remember sometimes it's best to sleep on it

A Stage Manager's Survival Guide: From Callbacks to Closing

before sharing it. When in doubt, I try to think that if someone were to say about me what I'd like to say about that person, how would I feel? Would I be willing to say it to the person's face? Not that it's always appropriate to resolve such things face to face, but I've found if it's not something I want the person to find out I said, don't say it. In the end, remember bad news travels significantly faster than good. So be mindful of the bad news you share. Also, be sure to share the good news! Tell the director about that actor who always stayed to help you clean up the rehearsal furniture, or tell the production manager about that spot operator who always showed up early and helped sweep the stage and assist the house manager. I found that when I have shared positive feedback, it often also makes my life easier, as those folks return as crew members for other shows. Primarily because they were good crew to begin with so the theatre wanted to hire them back, but also because they eventually heard I praised them for their work and they actively sought out the show I worked on as a result. In general, if you want people to say good things about you, it's best to say good things about others. Just be sincere and honest in any feedback shared.

SURVIVAL TIP #6: Embrace the chaos.

No matter how organized a director is, how detailed the rehearsal and tech schedule are, things will change. Actors will be sick and miss the night we blocked their entire act. Dancers will have tweaked an ankle and have to miss the night their big number is choreographed. Tech Sunday will come around, and only half of the light cues are ready and one of the speakers will have stopped working. It happens. Accept it, embrace it, and move on with life.

However, it is important that a stage manager anticipates as much as possible. You'll have checklists, scene breakdowns, shift sheets and every other form known to man. These are all important items to have, but they are one of a handful of the many tools for addressing the chaos. When whatever disaster happens, take a breath and focus on a solution. You'll have time later to run around and rant and scream how you can't believe the lead forgot the only

A Stage Manager's Survival Guide: From Callbacks to Closing

critical costume piece he has at home which he shouldn't have taken home in the first place.

I wouldn't say chaotic situations are fun, but in theatre (when no one is at risk of serious injury of course), they actually are. It is in those moments I get to see how creative I can be with problem solving. Duct tape and push pins will only get you so far. If you remind yourself there is ALWAYS a solution, you'll be able to see it. And implementing that solution can be very exhilarating.

When it comes to the chaos of cue calling, for some shows it is lights up and down and take a nap. Then there are the fun ones where you have over 300 light cues, 200 sound cues, and some projections too! While the technically complicated shows can make for a rather rough tech week, the thrill and rush of that moment when it all clicks and you call, or run, the perfect show... nothing can beat it. Same goes for nailing that set change where the whole thing rotates in a tiny space, or when that actor finally says every single word in the important monologue perfectly. Those are the moments when it is clear how much value a stage manager adds to a show. The conductor might bring the orchestra in line so each note sounds perfect, but when that curtain goes up, you bring EVERYTHING in line, and order to the chaos, so the whole experience is as the original vision for it was intended to be.

SURVIVAL TIP #7: Let your passion shine.

Stage management is a very demanding and often thankless job. Something you need to know, and tell yourself often, is that regardless of anything else, you are never "just a stage manager". You are A STAGE MANAGER! Shout it with enthusiasm from every mountain top! Take pride in your work and the gratitude and appreciation will follow. Don't just scribble a checklist off on a napkin. Print it out with all the thoughtful details noted and ordered in the most efficient way possible. Don't just throw your script around with a few scribbles of blocking on it. Take detailed blocking and notes, because when an actor comes to you asking about an entrance or when they cross somewhere, they'll notice how wonderfully you captured all of the blocking and appreciate that you helped them. When the lighting designer asks

A Stage Manager's Survival Guide: From Callbacks to Closing

at a production meeting if a space is used in a certain scene, and you have the answer at the tip of your fingers, they'll notice and appreciate the help. Embrace all of the details that go into stage managing a show well.

Remember, stage managing isn't for wimps. It takes a lot of energy and stamina, but find those moments that make it all worth it for you. For me, it can be the standing ovation on opening night, or hearing that an actor referred to me as their "stage manager extraordinaire" to people when I'm not in the room. One of my most memorable, was after stage managing a show with a large cast and a ton of coordinating of everything, I was feeling a bit unappreciated and frustrated as it seemed no one noticed all the work that went into making each show run smoothly. Until closing night. One of the actors sought me out to give me a beautiful plant, box of chocolates and "thank you speech" from the cast. It was so sincere and sweet, and a complete surprise. It was a reminder that even when you don't think people are looking or notice that you gave 110% of your heart and soul to the show, in the end, they have noticed and were grateful for every bit of it. Granted, that doesn't happen on every show, don't ever expect it. But in my career I've learned that some casts are better at expressing it than others. Just because they didn't give you a rose or thank you card doesn't mean they don't value all that you do and the passion you have for what you do. Because trust me, they do.

By: Michelle Marko, copyright 2015

A Stage Manager's Survival Guide: From Callbacks to Closing

Chapter 3: Auditions/Callbacks

And so it begins. You've secured the spot as stage manager for the show, congratulations! Now what? I've discovered that the journey truly begins with the auditions, or depending on the theatre, the callbacks. That glorious time when a stage manager has a chance to meet their future cast, and promptly forget all of their names because there are many more of them and only one of you!

SURVIVAL TIP #8: Listen to all. Share what is necessary.

This can be a fun filled day, as former actors you've worked with appear one after another, or as you have the pleasure to meet new people that you may or may not get the chance to work with. This is also a critical time for a stage manager to see through the façade of personalities. Everyone knows that an actor will put on the big smile and ooze massive charm when in the presence of a director, or anyone with casting power. However, that person who checked you in, took your conflict sheet and headshot, THEY get to see who the actor is when they're nervous and don't have the charm cranked up.

For example, when helping with callbacks for a large cast, I noticed an audition form didn't have an address listed. Upon asking the actor for the information, they responded with "I can't give you an address because there is a warrant out for my arrest". I smiled and said "ok. Thanks". Then at the first moment possible that wasn't completely obvious, went and told the director about this. She appreciated the immediate update, had them share their monologue, but excused them in the first round. That way the actor felt they were heard and walked away having a good experience with the theatre, and the show didn't end up casting what could have been a disaster. No one wants an actor to be arrested, no matter what the reason, on opening night, so the director was thrilled to avoid the mess all together.

A Stage Manager's Survival Guide: From Callbacks to Closing

    Another callback that stands out for me was for a very intense play with a large cast. The director, artistic director and a few others had been in the theatre watching actor after actor read from various pre-selected portions of the script. I had been doing my best to keep the chaos moving by shuffling one group after another in and out, occasionally remembering that the director might need a break. The day was drawing to a close and we were down to the last half dozen actors. While the director and others assisting with casting were debating and discussing what final bits they wanted to hear, the actors and I were sitting in the lobby. This is usually the time where people are either talking about other shows they've done or random small talk. For this callback however, there was one actor who sat there chatting intently with the actor sitting next to him about how he was a clear shoe-in for the lead and how he felt bad for anyone who had to read opposite the other guys up for the role because they didn't give as much to their scene partner as he did. He was dead serious and dead certain. I did my best to bite my tongue as the role had already been cast; the main character in this play was extremely intense and required months and months of prep work. This individual also bragged to have only read the play for the first time a few days before the callback. Yup. Shoe-in for the lead indeed.

    As the stage manager for the show, when everyone was discussing casting options, we came to that moment where the director asked me "do you have any comments or observations about the actors?" Now, more often than not, the people I observe as being the "problem children" are so obnoxious that the director sees it as well and has no desire to cast them. However, with a large cast there are plenty of ensemble roles that need filling. I'm a firm believer that a stage manager should not bias a director when casting. The director has a vision, and should be supported in casting that vision. As the stage manager who will be dealing with the resulting casting choices, and all of the drama that follows unfortunate casting choices, it's important to speak up about potential issue-causing actors. As such, my answer was simple. "In general, everyone was very nice. A few were a bit louder than others, but quieted down when alerted to their volume." I paused, with a big smirk on my

A Stage Manager's Survival Guide: From Callbacks to Closing

face causing the director to follow up with "Buuuuut." She knew that smirk meant I had some dirt to share. "One actor was very clear that we were very fortunate to be in his presence as he was clearly being cast as the lead," I offered honestly. We smiled, as we knew that role had been cast and the director thanked me for confirming her gut feeling about not casting him in a supporting role. I refrained from sharing further details about his general smugness. The arrogance he expressed by stating so boldly he was meant to be the lead accomplished the goal of alerting the director that he was a potential issue-causing actor. There was no need to share gossip or otherwise speak negatively about the person, because in the end my goal isn't to slander someone, but to help ensure the show will run smooth, and who knows, that person's bravado might have really been nerves. Perhaps that actor would be fantastic in another show. Don't ever assume they'll always be the same person. After all, I've certainly changed how I stage manage over the last 20 years.

While not all stage managers will attend auditions or callbacks, I highly encourage it and recommend attending them whenever possible, specifically the callbacks. That's typically when casting is discussed and decided, which for this impatient person means I don't have to wait to see who I'll be working with! I've always thought the moment a stage manager finds out who will be in their cast is like the joy of opening a present on a birthday. I love discovering who I'll be spending the next three months with, sharing in the artist adventure.

SURVIVAL TIP #9: Start off on the right foot.

Another benefit to attending callbacks is that you get a glimpse as to how your director works. Do they have a set schedule in advance? Do they prefer to sort it out as you go along? Do you find opportunities to help them, or do they seem to do it all themselves? What about the show or particular project excites them? There is no right or wrong answer to these questions, but you get the idea of what you can learn about your director at this early stage of the process.

A Stage Manager's Survival Guide: From Callbacks to Closing

Keep in mind; this is also a chance for your director to learn about you. Are you willing to do whatever odd job is needed to help keep the day running smoothly? Are you able to keep things organized? Are you eager to work with the director or do you try to take control of everything? Before arriving that day, at least 15 minutes early of course, think of how you want that first impression to come across. For musicals, do they imagine having a big ensemble, knowing you can only fit eight people backstage? For a technically challenging play, what do they envision for the "book magically appears from the ceiling" in a theater with no fly rail? What general concerns does the director have that you can help with or keep an eye on?

Don't focus all your energy on the director though. Remember that all those actors are important to get to know and make a good impression with as well! You might be the first person they interact with at the theatre that day. It's important to make everyone feel welcomed and do what you can to make them as comfortable as possible. Remember, unlike you, they don't have the role secured and are probably nervous. Offering a friendly smile and saying thank you when they give you the paperwork are small things you can do to help put them at ease. Building a good rapport with them during auditions or callbacks will only help make rehearsals run smoother and be more enjoyable.

A Stage Manager's Survival Guide: From Callbacks to Closing

Chapter 4: Production Meetings

With the casting complete, you will also be learning who the complete directing and design staff consists of. Ideally for larger shows, but not always needed for smaller shows, there will be a production meeting before the first rehearsal. This should be the first of many production meetings. If the theatre has a production manager, be sure to coordinate with them to see when the first meeting will be and who (either you or the production manager) will confirm and setup the first meeting. If you do not have a production manager, confirm with the director when they would like the first meeting to be. Then it will be up to you to reach out to everyone to make it happen.

SURVIVAL TIP #10: Take obsessively detailed notes.

Once at the meeting, it is critical that you take the most obsessively detailed notes that anyone has ever seen. These notes will be incredibly helpful for any of the design staff that aren't able to attend the meeting, or more likely, to remind them of an idea or thought that was said in passing and they forgot about. This includes such items as: discussions about color palettes, general set design ideas, music directions, and general feelings, thoughts and messages the director wants to convey. Don't feel bad if some of the notes seem silly or if people even say "Wow, that's a bad idea." I've had it happen more than once where I wrote something down, such as having a mirror ball magically appear to make the stage sparkle, and had everyone laugh at the joke only to later say that it was a brilliant idea. While in the end we didn't have an actual mirror ball used, by referencing that note, the lighting designer understood the look the director was trying to achieve and adjusted his lighting design to incorporate this.

I've also seen where a silly idea noted in a production meeting for *Angels In America* about a giant book flying up behind the house led to a serious discussion about how to technically have the giant book appear from a platform behind the audience. Ultimately this silly idea led to an ideal solution. It was a breakthrough because before the joke was made, we were stuck in thinking the book had to appear from upstage. Then someone said jokingly, "Wouldn't it be fantastic if it just POPPED OUT behind everyone and scared the crap out of them?" Had I not noted this down in the production meeting notes, the serious conversation at the next meeting which ultimately was what gave us a much needed solution might never have happened.

Additionally, detailed notes should include specifics about open items. Don't just list "need costume fittings by May 10". Be sure to list who is responsible for making sure those costume fittings happen by May 10th. Is it you? Will the costumer reach out to the actors? Is it someone else? Write it all down in a clear and easy-to-follow way. It never hurts to have an "open items" section in the meeting notes (such as in the example below).

Today's meeting: **Jun 16, 2014** 5:30 – 6:30pm	Present Ron, Jeff, Erin, Jennifer, Anna, Nick, Emily, Michael
Next meeting: June 23rd (Time TBD)	

GENERAL

For Camelot – the awnings are going away because otherwise people would knock it off or some such awful thing. Mylar gold shiny curtains will be downstage. Discussed Tim and where to put him, likely on top a turret w/ a fog machine (which does not move). So fogger sits in one place and dryer hose tubing runs it from one place to the other. He'll have ropes on him (though they are for the look and don't function).

Vegas wheels will potentially be motorized and move slowly.

OPEN ITEMS:
- Ron & Jeff to sit down and go through projections and such to confirm what is really needed. And then loop in Nick to see if the projections have to be in one place.

SCENIC
- The not yet dead cart: will have 5 bodies on the cart. It needs to be looong (vs. super wide).
- Giant bunny – will appear through house vom, with a tilting head so it can go through doorways.
  - Actors rolling the bunny on will also need to bring a ramp so it can get up on the stage.
- Hand of god: hidden behind permanent clouds hanging from the ceiling.

SURVIVAL TIP #11: Clarity with schedules.

Before the first meeting, you'll have confirmed with either the production manager or the Director who needs to reach out to schedule the meeting. While at the first meeting, be sure to talk to everyone about when the

A Stage Manager's Survival Guide: From Callbacks to Closing

next meeting should occur. The amount of meetings needed will vary for each show. I've had some shows where we only officially met twice as the director preferred to have many one-on-one meetings with designers. Or I've seen the opposite where we had a production meeting every other weekend with everyone there and no side-conversations outside of those meetings. Look to the director and designers to determine what is needed; the number of meetings is not up to you.

    A few important questions to ask at the first meeting about scheduling: When do we want the second meeting? When do we think the designer run should happen? When do we think paper tech should happen?

    It's also good to confirm the most efficient way to contact the designers with questions. Is it via the rehearsal reports, separate emails, phone calls, or some other method? Consistent and clear communication with the designers is extremely important during the rehearsal process. However, communication is only good if both parties see it. If you email everything to someone who only looks at their emails once a month, they won't receive important information and items could be built or designed that aren't what everyone else was hoping for or expecting. I once religiously emailed a prop designer about the real food needed in a holiday show with a big Thanksgiving dinner and included some specific food allergies the cast had. When it came time for tech, she showed up with the food as it was noted in the script. It wasn't what we were planning to use and included an item an actor was deathly allergic to. What happened? She no longer used that email address and never saw any of my emails. Had I double-checked her email address at the first production meeting, or noticed she never responded to my emails and followed up with a call, the time and money she spent on food wouldn't have been wasted.

SURVIVAL TIP #12: Don't panic!
    This is the first of many times I'll say this… Don't panic! During production meetings, many items are discussed that are typically the stuff of stage management nightmares. Set pieces appearing from the floor in a theatre

A Stage Manager's Survival Guide: From Callbacks to Closing

with no trap room, actors on roller skates on extremely steep ramps, large set pieces that spin around with actors on then for a set change, having actors magically teleport from one side of the stage to the other, or smoke machines EVERYWHERE. The list is endless. You have to remember that creating a show is an art form. Part of the art form is sharing ideas and not restricting your imagination. Listen and note down the ideas, but try not to panic. I still struggle with this myself as my lighting designer will often look over and see my cringing only to say "don't worry. It'll be fine by tech". I'm always quick to confirm, as while I may not always be able to hide my initial panic, I can confirm that I support the process with a simple and sincere "I'm not worried. You always make it easy to handle." The important thing is to allow the conversation and creativity to continue unhindered. I'm happy to say that in the end, I've never had a designer create something that I couldn't handle (although the steep ramp and roller skates was a close call… thank goodness for those wheelie sneakers!). It might have taken some cue calling practice or set change maneuvering, but it always worked out somehow.

A Stage Manager's Survival Guide: From Callbacks to Closing

Chapter 5: The First Rehearsal

Ah, that wonderful first rehearsal! It's like the first day of school. The first time everyone in the cast will be together to read through the play, sign tons of paperwork, and hear the director's vision of the show. More importantly, it's the first time you get to see everyone you'll spend the next few months with!! I always love re-uniting with former actors, directors and designers as well as trying like mad to learn the names of all the new faces. The moment when I walk in the door for that first rehearsal is still one of my favorite parts of the rehearsal process. At that moment, everything in a show is possible.

SURVIVAL TIP #13: It begins before the beginning.

However, there is still much to do BEFORE that moment. To start things off on the right foot, it is best to send an email to the cast before the first rehearsal. Even if a production manager has sent an email about the when and where, it would still be beneficial to send a reminder to the cast of the first rehearsal. Coordinate with the production manager and director as needed, but take a moment to let the cast see who you are before they walk through the door on the first day. It doesn't need to be long winded, just a simple note stating your excitement for the project, and provide them with your contact information. List out your email (don't assume they'll be able to reply to or see the address), your cell phone or whichever phone number you want them to call during rehearsals, and the best way to reach you with questions. Remember, this will be their first interaction with you, so make sure you are welcoming and informative. If this is their first show with that particular theatre, you want to make sure you give them a good impression of what it is like to work there.

There's a second portion to this tip though. You have a lot of preparation to do before walking into that first rehearsal. Make sure you have

A Stage Manager's Survival Guide: From Callbacks to Closing

a chance to chat with the director and production manager to confirm who will be doing what in terms of updating calendars, establishing the schedule, maintaining conflict sheets, scheduling the first production meeting, providing scripts for the cast, providing YOU with a script, etc. Take the time to put your prompt book, or Stage Manager's Bible, together. I often try to pick out different color binders to match the show such as red for Amadeus or green for Midsummer Night's Dream. It's just another way to make each show unique. And since you'll be carrying it around for a while, it might as well be pretty to look at. Get your tabs in order, and get your paperwork in order. The tabs you have will change over the years, but make sure to have the basics: one tab per act, pre-show, intermission, post-show, one tab for each design branch; and always one miscellaneous tab. It's good to include a tab for production meeting notes, contact sheets, schedules, and any other combination of tabs that are available in the standard Stage Management book (or internet search). As for the paperwork, have a blank rehearsal report, performance report and production meeting report ready to go and customized as needed for the show. Start thinking about what kind of run crew will be needed and how many assistants you would like. While you might not be able to choose the people for your crew or actually get the number of people you would like, the earlier you think about it and communicate it to the appropriate people in the office, the better off you'll be! I typically try to have my binder and reports ready to go at least one week before the first rehearsal. This gives me a week to remember all the things I might have forgotten. The other thing to prep is your stage manager kit, really this is just an excuse to go shopping and buy office supplies, first aid supplies and all the other random items you have to have on hand. Remember your kit should allow you to say "yes" to whatever someone might ask for. Typically, pencils, highlighters, paper clips, Band-Aids, gum, tape, and headache and allergy medicine are the most popular items. This can be a lengthy list of items that will vary depending on the theatre. An internet search might help you identify what will make the most sense for your show. Whatever the items, I strongly suggest going into the store with a list. On more

A Stage Manager's Survival Guide: From Callbacks to Closing

than one occasion I've walked into a store needing five items only to find myself walking out with five bags of stuff all for one show.

SURVIVAL TIP #14: Establish the ground rules.

On the day of the first actual rehearsal, be sure to ask the director for a few minutes to speak before digging into the read through or artistic talks about the show. Use these few minutes to establish the ground rules for rehearsals with the cast. For me this typically includes topics such as starting and ending rehearsals on-time, so they should show up a few minutes early. I'll also say how early I personally plan to be there so they know when they can expect doors to be open. If you're not the one unlocking the space, this isn't as critical to share but still helpful for them to know. It's about setting expectations from the beginning. This includes sharing what you expect from them and what they can expect from you. Let them know if there is a website, forum or phone number they should go to for information about schedules and any changes. Confirm that everyone in the cast is able to access your preferred means of communication. This is less common now, but 10 years ago, many people didn't have email. I would confirm at the first rehearsal who did and who was able to check it frequently. Anyone who didn't have email I had to call with any schedule updates or changes. When working with young cast members, make sure their parents are also able to access schedule information since they are often the ones having to transport the actor.

This is also the time to reinforce that putting on the production is a team effort. You're not there to be their parent or their janitor. Everyone needs to be responsible for themselves and respectful of each other's time and efforts. No one is more or less important in the production than anyone else. Mentioning this in a friendly and positive way at the first rehearsal sets the tone and can help minimize potential diva moments later on. This happened to me for multiple musicals with teen and adult casts. When one of the actors would start being overly self-centered, I would hear someone say "Hey, we're a team." Occasionally, I would be cheesy and even say "There's no 'I' in team or in (name of play)" if there wasn't an "I" in the title of the play. I'd hear them

A Stage Manager's Survival Guide: From Callbacks to Closing

saying it to each other in a playful way, but the message was received and a few actors who had diva moments in previous shows were kept in line.

SURVIVAL TIP #15: Your phone number must be their best friend.

With so much to coordinate, it's important the cast, directors, designers and house staff know how to reach you at all times. Typically, this means your cell phone number needs to be in all of their phones. Be sure to tell everyone what phone number they should use to contact you. I suggest listing it on the bottom of the calendar handed to them with a note about "Call me if you're running late @ 555-555-2345", but also I'm known to ask everyone to take out their cell phones and add my digits right then and there. Be sure to remind them that there is only one of you and many of them, so when texting for the first time it would be beneficial if they included their name. My favorite text in a rehearsal with a large cast is "I'll be 5 minutes late" with no name. In that situation, I don't respond with "who is this" because they are typically driving and I don't want to encourage them to text and possibly get in an accident. Instead, I'll pull out the contact list and see who the number belongs to. Or worst case; see who isn't there and who shows up five minutes late. Ta-da! Then I'll be sure to save the number with their name in my phone so next time I know who it is.

A Stage Manager's Survival Guide: From Callbacks to Closing

Chapter 6: The Rest of Rehearsals

With rehearsals underway, now the real fun can begin… the coordination, staging, digging into the meat of a play, or finding all the non-obvious moments to add humor… watching the show go from words on a page to real moments on stage. There is so much for a stage manager to do in this time that it can often be overwhelming.

SURVIVAL TIP #16: Laugh. Breathe. Take more notes.

Regardless of the type of production you are working on, there is always room for laughter in rehearsals. I've often found that the more intense the topic of the play, the more we tend to laugh in rehearsals. Mostly because being so intense for so long can be draining, it's important to find the appropriate moments to stop and laugh. When working on *Dead Man Walking*, I remember a few rehearsals where we laughed so hard my sides hurt. Yet within the same rehearsal I was also deeply moved and tearing up.

Additionally, the closer I get to tech week, the more stressed and tense things tend to be. This is when having a few websites, videos or other sources of humor can come in very handy. One of my favorites was during *Compleate Female Stage Beauty*, one of the actors was playing a YouTube video of British actors doing voices for animals. Rehearsal came to a complete standstill as we all stopped and watched, doubling over on the floor laughing. For the remainder of the show, folks would randomly quote the video and we'd all just laugh. During some stressful tech rehearsals, it was those quotes that kept a smile on my face and kept me from getting overly stressed. To this day, whenever I hear someone say, "Alan, Alan, Alan, Al, Al," I think of that cast and amazing show and smile. These days it is so easy to find a funny and random video or photo to share with the cast and designers, so don't hesitate to share them yourselves or encourage others to do so. Really it's about enjoying the time you have together, because in the blink of an eye the show will be closed

A Stage Manager's Survival Guide: From Callbacks to Closing

and you'll be moving on to your next project. Make sure throughout rehearsals to take a few moments here and there to laugh and enjoy being with everyone.

Of course not every rehearsal starts on time, ends on time and runs without a hitch. During the times when things are going sideways, stop and breathe. Even the WORST rehearsal will come to an end. I've had rehearsals where the lead showed up 45 minutes late. We all just had to sit around waiting for them because they were in every scene with the majority of the lines. There have been times when we couldn't get music to work for a dance rehearsal, and as this was before smartphones and everyone having laptops, it made for a chaotic and eerily quiet dance rehearsal.

A great example of needing to breathe was when an actor once yelled at me over the phone. He followed that up with extremely rude text messages before rehearsal. Then I had to spend four hours with him at rehearsal. In that situation, I stopped and took a big breath. When that wasn't enough to completely compose myself, I walked around the empty halls for a few minutes alone. Sometimes, you need to leave the physical space to just get your mind back in order.

During the first tech rehearsal for an extremely technical show set in space (oddly enough there have been more than one of these for me), we were stopping and starting frequently for one portion. I shouted out that we were going to reset the scene to run it again and heard from the stage, "I'm not ready. I need a few minutes." I've never had that happen before. An actor wanting tech to stop during tech! Being rather exhausted myself, I about lost it. After a moment of shock, I took a breath and got up, since we were clearly now on a break, and stepped outside for a moment. That breath allowed me to maintain a level head, well mostly anyhow, and continue on with the tech. For awhile after that moment, I was perturbed that the actor had the nerve to say what he did. But in looking back, in stopping to take that breath, I realized that when you have 80% of the lines in the show, that first tech rehearsal is going to be as mentally exhausting for the actor as it is for the stage manager, and I was proud of him for having the guts to speak up. Had I not taken that moment, and simply yelled or fought or done some other unproductive thing, there

A Stage Manager's Survival Guide: From Callbacks to Closing

would have been unnecessary tension and drama created. After all, the drama should be saved for on stage, not off. As a result, we had a great run and I really enjoyed working with the actor. He was appreciative of all that the crew and I did for him during the run, and I look forward to working with him again. This is a sentiment that could easily have gone the opposite way had I not stopped to breathe.

Laughing and breathing are great, but really to survive rehearsals you must take more notes than anyone normal ever would. Find your favorite medium for these notes, whether it's a laptop, pen and paper, special notebooks, tablets, or a variety of post-it notes. Explore different options and combinations until you find what works best for you. Having appropriately detailed rehearsal reports is extremely important and can save designers many emails or phone conversations, as well as keeping scheduling clear. The rehearsal report is also an important tool to keep track of who is on time and late, which is something the Production Office will greatly value, among others. Just be sure you are fair and consistent in noting down who is late or otherwise out. Don't play favorites, because while it seems like a small item at the time, noting or not noting that a particular actor is always five minutes late can impact their reputation with the theatre.

In keeping with the breathing suggestion, I will typically fill out my rehearsal report during rehearsal, but make sure I walk away from it for an hour or so before sending it out. Often times I'll have made a comment that was a bit too snarky, or downright rude. After having walked away from it, I realized wouldn't actually help the show in anyway, so I wisely remove it. I'd also discover that something I thought made perfect sense during rehearsal, sounded like gibberish to me an hour later. Not only do the notes need to be fair, but they must be clear to anyone who reads it, not just to you. Keep in mind that the rehearsal reports and any other notes you take will be your lifeline when an actor, director or designer comes up to you and asks, "Do you know what we said about..." Just like being able to answer yes to any question that starts with "do you have a ..." it's equally important you can answer, "Yes I do" to any question about things discussed during production meetings,

A Stage Manager's Survival Guide: From Callbacks to Closing

rehearsals, or about the show in general. You are *the* go-to person after all. Below is a sample portion of a rehearsal report:

```
6:00 – 6:23: Talked through changes        Late:
6:23 – 7:15: Blocked A1 S1                 none
7:15 – 7:25: break
7:25 – 8:35: Blocked A1 S3, S5, S6, S8     Accident/injury:
8:35 – 9:00: break                         none
9:00 – 10:00: worked top of show
10:00 end of rehearsal                     Conflicts
                                           none


Next rehearsal: Feb 17
Rehearsal: @ 7pm
```

GENERAL
Lisa updated Max and Mike on the set changes. Then blocked A1 S1. After a break, blocked A1 S3 starting at pg 10, then went to sc 5, then sc 6, sc8. Woohoo! Blocked all the Venticelli stuff for act 1. Max and Mike released at 8:35. After a break, worked Salieri's opening monologue. And did brief notes after it. Ran it again, then notes and cleaned up for the night. Great progress indeed tonight!! ☺

SCENIC (SET)
- none

PROPS
- A1 S3 – need 2 coins (Salieri gives them to the Venticelli)
- Period goblets. Would like to have one in Salieri's house on the cake table will always have water in it.

COSTUME & WIGS
- Salieri – will need a pocket in his A1 S3 coat.
- Venticelli both need pockets in their A1 coats.

LIGHTS & SOUND
- Pg 11/pg 13, will there be a certain light look for these "inbetween" scenes?
- Pg 17 – would love to take lights down to Salieri on DC and street lamps then come up. For going into Sc 6

SURVIVAL TIP #17: Be consistent.

There is a saying about how the only constant in life is change. That is almost true for the rehearsal process, but something else *should* be constant and consistent, the stage manager. Specifically, communication from the stage manager must be consistent. If you have told the cast they can expect to receive email updates, be sure to send the email updates. If you're using a website or phone line to keep people informed of the latest scheduling changes, make sure to keep it up to date! While this sounds easy, as you get closer and closer to tech week, and you have less time to sleep, let alone update a website, it is important to somehow find the time to make those updates. Keep in mind that while you have to be at every single rehearsal for the entire time, the cast might not need to be there. They're juggling rehearsals and work and life just as you are. The more notice they can be given about

A Stage Manager's Survival Guide: From Callbacks to Closing

schedules, the better. If it means staying up until 1am to make the updates or send the email, it's worth it. The alternative is having an irate actor at the next rehearsal, or worse yet, having the word get out that you're not a good communicator.

My personal preference in recent years is to use a website to keep the directors, designers and cast up to date. It's not fancy. A very basic design that has the core information needed. It's also something I can update from anywhere as long as I have an internet connection, and it's something they can all access from any computer or smart phone. I always make sure to include a timestamp of when I last made changes so it is clear if something has been updated or not. This doesn't prevent all of the "am I called tonight" questions, but it does minimize them significantly. I spend the first week hammering it into everyone's heads to check the website daily, and I love how a few weeks later I'll hear the actors telling each other to "check the website."

The same tip is also true for sending rehearsal and performance reports. Be consistent in the amount of information included in the reports, and be sure to send them out after every single rehearsal or show. I've heard a few new stage managers say, "Well I didn't send one because we didn't really do much." Trust me. From the cast and designer's perspective, this is *never* true. If you had rehearsal, something was accomplished and it's important the entire staff know what that something was. Even if it's simply, "blocked the first scene with a kitchen island from another set. We'll have to re-block once that set is gone." I'm sure it felt like nothing was accomplished, but when the director comes to you later and says, "When did we last work on this scene?" you'll have the answer in your report. Granted, more often than not my reports include mostly start and end times, plus a list of who attended and a sentence or two about what we did. You don't have to write a novel every night, but do be consistent in what you write, and more importantly, when you send them out. Keep in mind, if there is something in a performance report about a big set piece that needs fixing or half of the light grid died, it would be best to send that report out the same night and not wait until morning, as the set or lighting folks will need all the time they have to fix it.

By: Michelle Marko, copyright 2015

A Stage Manager's Survival Guide: From Callbacks to Closing

I've often found myself feeling stuck between a rock and a hard place when it comes to sending reports out at the same time every day. A few things that have helped are creating a calendar reminder each day, or, if things in the show and my world are completely overwhelming, I'll have the ASM send the report. Remember you have an assistant for a reason; don't be afraid to have them help with some of the day to day tasks you'll need to complete.

SURVIVAL TIP #18: "Thank you."

These two words are easy to forget to say, but noticed by others when they are not said. Remember that everyone working on this show is giving their time and energy to the production. Just like you, they likely had plenty of parties, concerts, outings, etc. they could have attended instead of rehearsal. At the end of each rehearsal, share your gratitude with a sincere "thank you" to everyone who was there. It doesn't matter if they sat in the wings the entire night because you didn't quite get to their scene. They were there. It doesn't matter if they showed up an hour late, said it was your fault they were late and generally made your life hell that night. They were there and contributed to the success of the show, so thank them. Now it is important to be sincere. Don't just pay the words lip service. This simple action can help bring a smile to someone after a tough rehearsal, or a long day. More than once, having the director say thank you as I was locking up and they were leaving brought a smile to my face because they took the time to notice I contributed that night.

The other side of this coin is remembering to say, "Please". A great stage manager knows how to delegate and how to ask for help. A key to people continuing to be willing to help is by treating them with respect and good manners. Don't just say, "Get me that gaff tape". You don't have to sugar coat everything either. "Could you please pass that gaff tape if you're not too busy" can quickly sound condescending and only upset someone. Remembering to talk to someone how you would like to be talked to and politely saying, "Can you please get the gaff tape for me?" will help keep a rehearsal moving along with everyone in a positive mood. At the end of every rehearsal, if you haven't said "please" and "thank you" multiple times, something is wrong.

By: Michelle Marko, copyright 2015

A Stage Manager's Survival Guide: From Callbacks to Closing

SURVIVAL TIP #19: The drama ends with YOU!

The wonderful thing about working with artistic people is that you get to see their creative talent and often view the world in a new way. However, this also comes with a decent dose of drama, and not the kind you want. As a stage manager, it is critical that you are part of the drama solution and not the propagator of rumors. You need to be the person that everyone in the production is comfortable coming to with their concerns. Whether those concerns are valid, such as crew members getting a little too intimate backstage, or less critical, such as being out of strawberry flavored Laffy Taffy in the green room. You have to be able to hear whatever the concern is, and decide what the best course of action is. In the case of the Laffy Taffy, I suggested the actor pick up more candy the next day. In the case of the backstage crew fooling around, I started by talking to the crew members directly. When that wasn't enough, I had to escalate the issue to the production management. I had made the call not to escalate it immediately as I wanted to give the crew members every benefit of the doubt. Perhaps they didn't know how their actions made others feel, or that it was why they were missing a cue. As their stage manager, it was my goal to provide a safe environment for the cast but to also support my crew as much as made sense. Situations like that can be delicate though, and your course of action will vary depending on the details and how the theatre operates. When in doubt, always talk to the production manager or artistic director to get their input.

Regardless of the intensity of the drama, it is up to you to resolve it swiftly, professionally and respectfully. It is also important that you don't vent, rant, blab or otherwise gossip about it to other people in the production. Remember, you are your reputation (more on that soon). While many of the whispers still happen, it is a small and close-knit community, it's important that everyone can trust you to keep things professional. If someone comes to you with an issue, they need to trust that it will stay with you and not be blabbed to everyone. Often times, when dealing with some of the more ridiculous requests, such as during a youth production of *Guys and Dolls*, having a young male actor steal the shoes of a young female actor he liked, you'll really *want*

By: Michelle Marko, copyright 2015

A Stage Manager's Survival Guide: From Callbacks to Closing

to tell everyone because it's just funny, but fight the urge. That's what storytelling years later is for, to laugh about the silly things. It's equally important not to take sides. The stage manager should be the peacekeeper and as neutral as possible. This can be tough when there is drama between two individuals involved in the show, but treat them both with respect and fairness.

Sometimes the best course of action is to pretend you don't know a thing. I've found over the years when it comes to show-mances or other dating gossip between cast members, it's best to keep my nose out of it. I try to be aware of who is involved, just so I can keep an eye out for potential issues during the run, but in terms of details, I stay out of it. This has allowed me to stay neutral. For example, when working on a young adult show with a large cast, a particular actor was first dating one actress at the start of rehearsals, and by opening was dating another actress. Having not been involved in the daily scoop of what went on, I was able to stay neutral, listen to both sides of their story when any issues arose, and ultimately made sure the two females were at opposite ends of the dressing room for the run. No one in the cast knew that was why people were placed the way they were. It was a big room and I was able to justify the positioning with something about the order of costume changes. Really though, I had them strategically located. Fortunately this, combined with the two females being professional about things while in the theatre, did the trick and everyone had a wonderful run. Some of the stories about conversations outside of the theatre were a very different story. At the end of the show, I was proud that the backstage drama wasn't reflected on stage, that all of the people involved felt comfortable coming to me to voice concerns, and that I was aware enough of what was happening to anticipate some issues and resolve them before anything escalated. Fortunately, that was the most extreme case I've come across, so I wouldn't expect you'll have this happen often, but I have had issues between two people in a show arise often enough that the lesson I learned then has served me well.

A Stage Manager's Survival Guide: From Callbacks to Closing

SURVIVAL TIP #20: Stick it to them by taking the professional high road.

No matter how hard you try, there will be situations where you struggle to get along with someone involved in the show. This can be a particular struggle when it is one of the cast or crew. In those situations, take the professional high road! It will be tough, and trust me, you'll have moment where you'll want to join in the food fight and mudslinging, but don't. Fight that urge with everything in you! However, don't be a push-over. You do have options. For example, the rehearsal report. This can be a strategic way of communicating the core issue without making it a personal issue. However, make sure you are being honest and fair. Keep the language and items listed professional, but you can note things like rehearsals starting late because a certain actor got lost for the 5th time or simply forgot they were called that night. Remember the rehearsal report is read by all of the staff involved in the production and is a way to get things "on the record".

Have a classic "diva"? You can take the high road by treating them fairly at all times, but firmly and professionally. Others involved in the production will see how they respond to you. Be sure that you truly listen to what they say though. While it might be shared in an over the top way such as screaming from backstage ("Oh my God we have to stay in the costumes for ANOTHER TWO HOURS??? It's so damn hot we're going to all be dead!"), at heart they might have a problem that needs solving. In that case, it was finding a fan for the green room because the period costumes everyone wore cause most of the cast to overheat during the first tech rehearsal which happened to be on a really hot summer day. Often times, even if there isn't anything to solve immediately, letting them know that you listened to what they had to say can calm them down and prevent such "diva moments" from re-occurring.

Also, try to remember attitude is often a matter of perception. What you see as someone being a diva and acting obnoxiously, might actually be someone going through a rough time in their life. Perhaps they are facing a personal struggle at work or home; perhaps they just lost a loved one. Try to understand things from their perspective before assuming they are simply being a diva. I had a situation where a simple text completely changed an

A Stage Manager's Survival Guide: From Callbacks to Closing

actor's attitude. It was for a holiday play that wasn't a holiday musical, which for this actor meant he was 100% out of his musical theatre comfort zone. He had been struggling with the lines and generally with how to approach one of his characters, as a result of the struggles he started doubting himself and completely lost his confidence. The director saw this and worked with him; she was fantastic and was able to repair most of his doubts. However, one week before tech he started slipping into some of his previous bad habits. There was one scene in particular he really struggled with. A few nights before tech, he really nailed that scene. The rest of the night was a bit rough, but that one scene – he just completely nailed it. After rehearsal I sent him a text saying "Way to seriously kick ass on the scene tonight!!! I laughed so hard my sides were hurting." I sent that text because I remembered that night how he struggled with adjusting to being in a play verses a musical, and I was really proud of how hard he worked to overcome it. Having worked with me for a few months, he knew that I'm not someone to say things I don't mean or to ever kiss ass. So when I give a compliment, it is 100% sincere. The next night he was back to his confident self and the show was back on track. I know it wasn't just my text that caused the change, but based on his reaction and change in mood, I know it helped in some small way.

SURVIVAL TIP #21: You are your reputation.

It's important to remember that stage managers don't audition; you have a resume and your reputation. Keep this in mind when dealing with tense or unpleasant situations or people. Before you send that sassy email that we all would LOVE to send where we tell that actor exactly where they can stick it, think about how this reflects on you. How would someone else perceive that email? The yelling match that you're about to initiate because your entire crew seems incapable of reading a shift sheet, is that really how you want to be known? If you heard that about someone else, would *you* want to work with them? Stage managers walk a fine line when it comes to attitude. There is a time and place to be firm with people, but as much as possible, be professional about it.

By: Michelle Marko, copyright 2015

A Stage Manager's Survival Guide: From Callbacks to Closing

Stage managers are people too and sometimes you'll have a moment you'd like to take back. I've certainly had my fair share over the years. Fortunately, a reputation is based on MANY moments so don't let one bad one keep you down. Brush it off, focus on a solution and on making the next rehearsal or performance wonderful. When I stage managed my first few shows after college, I know now that I came in with my attitude blazing which caused friction with the producers a few times. Fortunately, they were wise enough to understand I was still figuring out how things worked and didn't take it personally, because when I look back, I'm honestly impressed that they didn't bonk me on the head with a clue-by-four a few times when I insisted things be scheduled a certain way, or strike *had* to occur a certain way when I was completely incorrect. However, I was always hard working and made sure all my energy went into having the best show possible. The producers saw that potential in me and were able to look past my initial obnoxious behavior. Even stage managers can be divas after all. But you can turn that attitude around and be a stage manager who is known for working hard, getting the job done, having a positive attitude, generally is fun to work with, and always looking to improve. I'm not perfect and still have plenty of moments where I have to keep all of these tips in mind, but the turning point for me was when I realized the value of my reputation. After all, theatre is a close-knit community filled with people who are passionate about their art and want to produce the most amazing shows possible. Having the reputation of being someone who helps, instead of hinders, that process will get you farther than anything you can write on a resume.

A Stage Manager's Survival Guide: From Callbacks to Closing

Chapter 7: Tech Week

There comes a time in every show where you have to make the leap from rehearsals to full tech. No matter how prepared you are, how much you have planned every little moment, or how simple you think a show is, tech week is always an intense time of change. Personally, I think it's also one of the most exhilarating weeks as you really start to see the show take shape!

SURVIVAL TIP #22: Paper tech will keep you sane.

Before setting foot in the theatre on that first day of tech, make sure you have coordinated a paper tech with your sound and lighting designer! I also strongly recommend having the director there. I have had a few musicals where the director wasn't able to attend paper tech, but they had met with the designers extensively beforehand so everyone was on the same page. Depending on the theatre, the production manager might also want to attend. I would suggest talking about paper tech and when best to have it early on in the production. This will ensure that lights and sound is clear on what their deadlines are and that they have the proper time needed to actually build all of the cues needed. I've only had one show were the light cues weren't ready for tech Sunday, and it was the most painful tech day we as a team ever had. The frustrating thing for me is that it could have been avoided if I had coordinated the paper tech better.

While at the actual paper tech, be mindful of the time. Especially for shows where you've worked with the director or designers before, it is very easy to get sidetracked and start chatting about everything besides the actual cues, or to get into an intense discussion about the opening music and lights going out together or feeding off each other, etc. Try to keep the conversations focused and productive. I've been known to say, "Well let's start with it this way, and we can adjust it when we run it…" to try and resolve the "which goes first" discussions. Often times with a visual and audio medium, you really won't

A Stage Manager's Survival Guide: From Callbacks to Closing

know until you see and hear it. That's why we have tech week. No need to get stuck on that during paper tech.

If possible, have the paper tech on a different day from the first day of tech. This gives the designers that little extra time to implement any changes discussed during paper tech and to otherwise fine tune cues. This also gives you a chance to absorb what you'll need to be calling. Although I do strongly, and I mean STRONGLY, recommend giving yourself one full day of "no theatre" before going into tech week for your personal mental sanity. Sometimes this means paper tech will be the Friday before a tech Sunday. Or it might violate my suggestions and be early in the morning of tech Sunday. If you think paper tech will take less than 2 hours, doing it the morning of is fine, just be aware that you'll really have to keep folks focused to finish up as quickly and efficiently as possible. For musicals, Shakespeare, or long shows like *Amadeus*, accept the fact that it won't be a "quick-and-easy" paper tech and schedule it for a day other than the first day of tech.

SURVIVAL TIP #23: Be prepared. Then prepare some more.

For a stage manager, there is no such thing as being too prepared for tech week. I've found that a great way to make sure I don't forget what preparations are needed in my sleep-deprived tech mind is to create a checklist. I'd suggest creating the checklist in-between working on shows so you have time to really stop and think about every single possible thing to include. If you have this list, then preparing and knowing you are as prepared as any human stage manager can be will set you up to succeed. I've had more than one show where early on, before I had my checklist, I was convinced I had everything ready. Band-Aids? Check. Shift sheets? Check. Highlighters for crew to use on shift sheets? Check. Prompt book? Check. Contact numbers? Check. Laundry reminder to cast and crew? Check. Actually doing my own laundry? Ooops. Taking time off of my day job for particularly long shows, especially when fighting a cold? Hmm, nope. I paid the price for that one on *Guys and Dolls* by getting a VERY bad case of pneumonia in the middle of tech week.

A Stage Manager's Survival Guide: From Callbacks to Closing

Vitamin C or cold prevention items was promptly added to the list after that show as was requesting at least two days off of my day job.

The important thing to note is that preparation for a stage manager extends beyond the theatre. The following are some of the items I now list on my checklist to help me prepare. Everyone will have their own unique items, but hopefully some of the below will help get you thinking about what will be important for you to include.

- Send email to cast, designers, and crew with the following:
    o The rough schedule for Tech Sunday
    o Expectations of everyone during tech
    o Reminder to do laundry and grocery shopping in advance
    o Reminder to be respectful, patient and kind
- DO YOUR OWN LAUNDRY (especially darks)
- Buy food for the week
- Confirm prompt book is ready
- Have fresh highlighters for others to use
- Print out shift sheets for crew
- Print out props lists to posts on each side of backstage
- Print out props list to post inside prop cabinet
- Print out costume changes for green room
- Print out sign-in sheet
- Print out scene/musical list for green room
- Print out any sound/lighting cue sheets for you and crew
- Have pen/pencil on string and push-pin for sign-in sheet
- Have tape, pen, paper for covering and labeling prop tables
- Re-stock items in SM kit
- Check expiration dates on any medicine in SM kit
- Locate your spike, gaff and glow tape
- Make copies of scripts for crew

A Stage Manager's Survival Guide: From Callbacks to Closing

- Get at least 10 hours of sleep before Tech Sunday
- Set alarm with enough time to stop for coffee on the way to Tech Sunday
- Stock up on SM snacks for tech week
- Confirm vacation/days off from day job (especially Thursday and Friday mornings)
- Have spare charger for phone
- Have power plug/charger for laptop
- Think through the show: what odd items might the cast or crew need? (knee pads, pillows, fake blood, baby wipes, ear plugs, etc.)

While most of the tech week preparation is focused on making sure you can meet the needs of the cast and crew, the most important item above is actually about making sure that YOU are taken care of. Get sleep. I try extremely hard to make sure I have one full day, either Friday or Saturday, of no rehearsal or need to set foot in the theatre before I go into tech. This gives me a day to take care of all the above items, but to also make sure I have a night of solid sleep. Life doesn't always allow for this, but I've found when I'm able to get even that one night of good sleep before tech, it can make all the difference in my ability to handle stress and keep things productive and positive on that first 12-hour day. The more you are able to prepare before tech starts, the more time you'll be able to focus on calling the show, improving scene shifts, and generally have a smoother tech. Don't leave all of this prep for the day before though! Stressing yourself out before a week of stress doesn't help anyone, and is more likely to burn you out before you even get to lunch on the first day of tech. Do as much prep as early as you can, but know that many of the lists and such will be revised or created last minute because you simply won't know the details before then.

Regarding the email, I have a few email templates I use depending on the type of show (musical or play) which saves me the energy of having to remember what I want to include, during a time when I'm likely rather tired, and allows me to still send a friendly email in the appropriate tone. To create

A Stage Manager's Survival Guide: From Callbacks to Closing

the template, take an email sent from a show you worked on, or put yourself in the crew, cast, and designer's shoes to think of what would be helpful for them to receive. Just like the very first introduction email you sent to everyone, this tech week email will set the tone for tech. "You had better show up on time and be ready to stop A LOT..." is probably not the best approach. Go with something along the lines of: "Be prepared for pauses and start/stops, and please note we have a long day ahead of us. The earlier and more on-time we start, the earlier we can go to sleep!"

SURVIVAL TIP #24: Pad the time table!

I have found that the worst feeling in the world is to be approaching hour 12 of the first day of tech and to not have completed an entire run of the show. Having to hear the director say, "Ok, we'll pick up from this point tomorrow and then also run the full show" caused plenty of audible groans and other signs of exhaustion from the cast, crew, designers, and well, everyone. Sometimes that is just how it goes, but a stage manager can do their best to avoid this situation with one simple trick: pad the time allotted for everything on the first day of tech! For example, if you have a play like *Complete Works of Shakespeare Abridged*, which isn't a lengthy play but has a massive amount of props and costume changes, don't look at the run time as what you'll need for the cue to cue. Instead of thinking act 1 will take you one hour because that is how long it has run all through rehearsals, pad that time table because you'll have to start and stop and re-do and re-re-do changes. You have to feel it out, and when in doubt it's good to talk to the director to see what they think, but for *Complete Works*, I planned two hours for Act 1. We ended up using the full two hours, but it was a relaxed pace. The lighting designer was able to dramatically adjust their design to meet the director's needs on the fly. The crew was also able to sort out what I can only call "prop-ageddon" as they figured out the best cubbyholes and places to put each item. Having time to try different locations carefully is important when you have a giant inflatable T-Rex that must avoid sharp pointy things lest he pop.

Building in extra time for each item on the schedule is also the best way to make sure that you will have time for two of the most important things in life: food and bathroom breaks. This extra time is what will also ensure your lighting designer and sound designer have time for these two critical items as well. They are the easiest things to forget, and the most frustrating when you have to pause because the lighting designer is about to faint from not eating for 20 hours or because you have to run to the restroom as the 3 giant sodas you drank earlier caught up with you. It's silly, but those unscheduled breaks or pauses can throw off everyone's rhythm and cause general frustration. During one tech for a space musical, sodas caught up with me and I went for a quick break. On my way back out to the tech table, I passed by a few actors in a hallway who thought I was out of earshot. Needless to say, I heard the comment of "Geeez. Why didn't she take care of that during our last break like the rest of us did? Now how late are we going to have to stay?" There are many retorts to that, however if I were in their shoes, I would have likely thought the same thing. Taking the "unscheduled breaks" can be seen as disrespectful of everyone's time, and that is not the best way to start off a tech week.

SURVIVAL TIP #25: Everything changes.

No matter how beautiful your tech schedule is, or how much padding and planning went into it, know that one thing will always be true: everything will change. You thought giving the cast an hour and a half for wigs and make-up would be enough? Nope. I've had period shows where the females needed two hours to curl their hair. Oddly enough, when we dealt with wigs, we actually needed less time, so after a few grumbles of showing up two hours ahead and being bored, I was able to adjust call time to only one hour before curtain. Schedules are only the first thing to change though. Cues will change over and over again. I'm always excited when the last tech rehearsal before preview doesn't have any light or sound cue changes. I'm excited because that's only happened to me about five times in 20 years. This is why you never write your cues in pen. Ever! Even after opening.

These changes go beyond cues and schedules though. That set change you had neatly planned out that the director wanted to completely change because it didn't "flow right", don't worry. Try a few different options. I've had

A Stage Manager's Survival Guide: From Callbacks to Closing

a few variety or one act shows where the directors wanted the furniture to "dance on and off". In the end they realized they could have a smooth efficient scene change or one that involved all the pieces dancing but also took five minutes. The scene changes are an important part of the overall look and feel of the show, so depending what the director wanted, either of those options would work. Fortunately for my sanity, they chose the efficient option. So I was able to avoid trying to make a couch, that couldn't be wheeled on, beautifully appear.

The key to surviving all of these changes is to take it one moment at a time, not to panic, and listen to what is really being asked for or changed. Perhaps the director is pretty sure doing the lights and sound in reverse will look awful but they just need to see and hear it for themselves to confirm it. Take the 10 minutes and let them see it. Perhaps the costume designer forgot the lead had to do a complete change in two minutes while exiting one side of the stage and entering on the other side. The solution there was not to have the costume change take place completely in one location, but to have bits and pieces of it happen all through the cross backstage. Pants in one place, shirt in another, hat and belt in a third location. This allowed the actor to make the change and entrance and not feel panicked. It took us a few tries and adjustments to find the right combination and location for this. Had I not been open to change, I'm sure the actor would have made it work, but he would have been stressed out and since he was playing an extremely intense role, it would have impacted his performance. Additionally, I would have been stressed out every night wondering if he'd make the change on time.

SURVIVAL TIP #26: You set the mood.

Which leads me to the next tip. You as the stage manager really set the mood for tech week. It's an easy thing to forget as you're likely focused on other things such as cues, where the cast is, getting the crew up to speed, etc. However, try to remember that at all times how you react and act will impact the cast, the crew and the designers. If you come in to each tech rehearsal with a chip on your shoulder, you're more likely to snap at people and generally be

A Stage Manager's Survival Guide: From Callbacks to Closing

unpleasant, causing a trickle-down effect that results in everyone being tense, grumpy and generally unhappy. That's about the worst environment ever to create a piece of art.

Do your best to come in to each tech with a positive attitude. No matter how good or bad things went the day before, this rehearsal is a new opportunity for things to go well. Granted, it might not be the show causing your grumpy mood. I've had plenty of times where a rough day at work leaves me in a grump only to head off to tech rehearsal. I do my best to drop the grump. Sometimes I sit for a few minutes in my car listening to a favorite song, or I'll call or text a good friend before rehearsal starts to vent. Other times I'll grab my assistant before we start and say, "Hey, can I rant a bit about work?" At the least, I'll take a moment before I enter the building, pause and take a breath. Whatever works best for you, do that. The important thing is after the rant, or the breath, or the few minutes in my car, I was able to shake off that black cloud and start tech with a positive attitude.

There is the expression "Fake it until you make it." While some might suggest just faking a smile, I disagree. If you truly have things going on that you're not able to shake off, talk to your assistant and director. Let them know what is going on. During one tech I found out I was being laid off from my day job. This was extremely stressful news and while I wasn't in a bad mood, I certainly wasn't in a cheerful one. I pulled the director aside and told him, as well as the cast since there were only two of them. They were extremely supportive and while rehearsal continued on as normal, they gave me a little space at breaks and such. Basically giving me a few days to come to terms with things. By opening I was back to my usual self largely due to the support and understanding of the cast and director. I did my best to keep a positive attitude, and they understood when I wasn't my usual jovial self.

It's also important to remember that you are human. This is why I suggest *do your best* to have a positive attitude, and be aware of how your mood impacts others. Sometimes, you'll snap. This is where an assistant can really save the day! In the last few shows I've done, I've had the pleasure of working with the same amazing assistant stage manager. We're old friends and

A Stage Manager's Survival Guide: From Callbacks to Closing

he knows that I'm really not an evil person, I just have my stressed out moments. Just as important as it is for me to be aware of my attitude, it is equally important to have a solid relationship with your assistant. While it's not appropriate to dump all of your issues on them, after all you are the stage manager and the drama stops with you, I have found time and time again that having a great and trusting relationship with my assistant can help me get through the moments when my attitude is less than stellar. Either by then listening to me, or more importantly, by them saying, "Hey. What's your issue today?" The funny thing is the times when I'll appear to be in a bad mood but am just deep in thought about how to fix a set change or some other issue. I'll be staring at a paper VERY focused, but my ASM is saying things to help remind me that even when I'm in a good mood, I need to be aware of how I appear. One show with multiple one acts that had seemingly simple set changes comes to mind. The set changes ended up being incredibly complicated due to a lack of backstage space and a variety of large couches wheeling on and off for each one act. During tech, we were coming back from a break and I was standing on stage with the shift sheet, wandering in circles, waving my hands on occasion, and I hadn't given my usual call for the end of break. Really I was just focused and visualizing the different changes and some ideas in my mind. What my cast, director, and assistant saw when they came back was my intense thinking face and occasional mutterings and waving of arms. Basically, they thought I was mad at them about something. My assistant came up to me and asked, "Are we in trouble?" I gave her a puzzled look and said, "Uhm. No. I'm just trying to figure out how to fix this set change, and I keep getting stuck with the new couch on the wrong side. It's driving me nuts." The cast heard this and laughed, because I looked down at my watch and realized we were back from our break and I forgot to do my usual "come on back to the party" end of break call to the cast. I promptly smiled and called places and we continued on with rehearsal. I was grateful that my assistant said something because had she not, the rehearsal would have proceeded with an air of tension, which no tech rehearsal needs.

A Stage Manager's Survival Guide: From Callbacks to Closing

SURVIVAL TIP #27: Know when to follow the plan and when to go with the flow.

For most shows I've worked on in recent years, and every musical I've ever worked on, there is always that "one section" of chaotic cues. On occasion it has been more than one section, but there is always that one in particular that I find myself saying, "if I can just nail this tonight, all is well". This is inevitably the section during tech that will cause the most frustration for myself, and often others. Especially during the first cue to cue. That is when the director first sees the lights, sound, and scenery all together. It's also the first time I will be calling the cues. Oddly enough, it's not perfect. While I'll know what the lighting and sound designer are trying to achieve, finding that timing and when to call it, when to hit the button, is what tech week is all about. Now I know this. And I know I'll get it right before we have an audience, but my knowing this is useless. Everyone else needs to see and hear it for themselves. Which often means running and re-running and re-re-running specific sequences time and time again. Many times this is necessary to fine-tune and helps both the stage manager and the director get on the same page. Sometimes this delay can threaten to delay the entire tech schedule. It is important to know when you need to push back because of the rehearsal schedule and when you just need to go with the flow.

I've found that a director typically wants to run that one tough sequence about one or two more times than I'd initially like to during the early days of tech. Yes, it always throws the schedule off a little, but I'll typically pad the timetable so it doesn't completely throw the day off. Often times, if it's not the director wanting to see it "just one more time", it'll be the designer who needs to see how that looks or sounds. When this happens, take a breath, and do the sequence again. If there's specific reasons why you're not able to nail it 100%, share it with them honestly, but politely. "I need to go back two pages for the sound cue to be properly implemented," or "I can't see when the actor is set because the set change cue is darker than it will be," or "it's going to take some practice to execute this sequence exactly, but I understand what you're trying to achieve. Fresh eyes and energy tomorrow will do the trick". The key is

A Stage Manager's Survival Guide: From Callbacks to Closing

to communicate while being honest, respectful and professional. After saying some of the above I've had directors reply with "Oh, wonderful. I just wanted to make sure you knew what was supposed to happen when. We'll try it again tomorrow," or "No problem, let's go back to where it makes sense for you to call the cue," or "I understand, but I still really need to see it again for myself".

Remember that while you are often the conductor of the technical orchestra, you are not the center of the universe. I've often learned in post-rehearsal chats that the reason the director or designer wanted to see it that "one more time" wasn't because of a cue going right or wrong, but because they had an idea about some aspect of that moment and they were visualizing it in their mind. Having the sound, set and lights doing roughly what they should when they should was needed to help them better visualize the moment. Just as you need time to practice the cues and the crew needs time to practice set changes, the designers and director need time to fine tune their contribution to this piece of living art. I had one show with a set of a family room; on stage right was a partial wall and a screen door that lead to the porch. At the start of tech, the screen door was in one location, a location that happened to block some of the audiences view in a way that didn't appear on paper. However, as soon as we had the physical door and ran the cue to cue, the set designer and director quickly realized there was an issue. No problem! Just move the door, right? Heh. Well that's what we did, but then the lighting designer had to modify their design which also led to a few changes in the light cues. I was fortunate to be working with a wonderful director, cast and design staff so all of the changes were made with a laugh and a smile. A big part of that was because everyone was able to go with the flow, myself included. Yes this threw off the schedule for the day, but it was a critical issue that needed to be solved immediately. By giving the designers time to move the door and adjust the lights, we were ultimately able to carry on and still have a great tech rehearsal. Had I been rigid and refused to extend the dinner break so they could fix things, we would have had a miserable rest of the rehearsal and I'm sure many unproductive and unprofessional arguments would have happened. While it is the stage manager's job to keep things on schedule, it is also their

A Stage Manager's Survival Guide: From Callbacks to Closing

job to do so in a practical and productive way. During tech, "on schedule" simply means getting through each day having done a bit more than the day before. Sometimes that means getting through only Act 1. Sometimes it means running the show twice. All of it means being flexible and understanding why someone might need more time and knowing when that reason is important for the show and when it's something that can be dealt with at another time.

SURVIVAL TIP #28: Take care of your crew.

I feel like this is one of the most obvious tips, yet I've worked on shows as crew where this didn't take place, so clearly it's not as obvious as I thought. Now taking care of your crew means many things, however it does not mean that you have to be their best friend. You are their stage manager and leader. Although I have found that becoming friends with my crew makes the show more enjoyable for me and hopefully for them. I do my best to always maintain a level of professionalism and never to rant or vent, because quite frankly dumping my problems onto the crew makes things awkward for them and is just not a good practice.

So what does taking care of them mean? For me, it's making sure they understand what they'll be contributing before tech even starts. Assuming you know who your crew will be prior to tech week, invite them to watch a run through or stumble through. Remember, for most crew, they spend the entire time backstage and unless there are monitors, they won't ever have a chance to see what actually happens on stage. Watching a rehearsal can show them what the audience will see and also give them a sense of timing for the show and what they'll do. If they're doing set changes, seeing how many there might be is helpful. If they're doing costumes or props, seeing where and what happens can be a huge help, especially if there are a significant amount of quick changes. An additional benefit to having your crew attend a rehearsal is that you get to meet them before tech, and they get to meet you. Typically if you want to see a stage manager at her most pleasant, don't meet her on the first day of tech where she is likely incredibly stressed out. I've also had a crew person realize how many performances there would be on school nights. Since

A Stage Manager's Survival Guide: From Callbacks to Closing

she was a senior in high school, the Wednesday night and Thursday night performances were an issue. Because we were able to review the schedule before tech week, the production manager had time to find a replacement. There were no hurt feelings, and she ended up crewing the summer show when school wouldn't be a conflict. Had I not invited her to a rehearsal, we would have discovered the scheduling issue during tech week and things would have been much tenser.

In addition to inviting the crew to a rehearsal, on the first day of tech I make sure to have a copy of the script, calendar and contact sheet for every member of the crew. I don't care if they're a spot op, a prop runner, run crew, or anything else. If they are backstage or in the booth and working on the show as my crew, they get a copy of the script. I've always made a big deal out of this because I had a few shows in college that I ran spot for, but never received a copy of the script. It made me so sad because I loved the shows and wasn't always able to find the script on my own. It was also frustrating because during tech, when we would jump around or slowly go through an act, I had no idea of how much longer we had in a scene, or in general where we were in the show. You have to remember that while you've been staring at the script for months, the crew hasn't. In most shows, they've likely never read or seen the play before coming to tech. Giving each crew person a script is also a subtle way to help them feel like they belong and are a part of the show. Since the crew are added towards the end of the process, it's often easy for them to feel excluded or "just the crew". Having a script is one way to make sure they know you think of them as "your crew" and not "just your crew". Of course, if you're not able to have a full script for each of them, make sure to at least have a scene/character breakdown. Basically when someone says, "Let's run the baby Yeti scene," it's good for the crew to have some way of knowing when that scene happens in the show. Otherwise, you'll lose precious tech time telling them what needs to be set and when the scene happens.

Another easy thing to do to help the crew feel a part of the show is to make sure the cast is aware of what they are contributing. Perhaps before starting the first cue to cue, take a moment to say, "This is Suzy, she'll be

A Stage Manager's Survival Guide: From Callbacks to Closing

helping with quick changes. This is Tina and Tom, they'll be on spot". You don't need to share life stories, but let everyone know who those new people are, and don't be afraid to ask the cast to welcome them. Something as simple as, "'I'd like to welcome the crew to our *Dead Man Walking* family" can help everyone settle in that much faster. It also sets the tone that the crew is welcomed and appreciated.

    Lastly, just as you've done in rehearsal with the cast, remember to say "please" and "thanks" to your crew. No matter how intense or insane the tech rehearsal was, be sure to thank each and every crew member for their participation and help that day, especially on the first day of tech! The crew will have had to get to know the entire cast, figure out what they're doing for the show, and dive in on the most stressful day of the production. When I've been in the crew, having the stage manager come over and say, "Thank you for being awesome today," helped wash away a lot of the stress I might have felt, simply because I was appreciated.

    In general, I have found whether I'm on the crew or stage managing, when a stage manager takes care of their crew, the crew will take care of the stage manager. This can include showing up early to sweep and mop the stage, bringing some little sweet treat or coffee for the stage manager, offering to help update shift sheets or just hand them out, giving me a big hug and smile when they arrive, or asking to run a set change with just the crew before the cast arrives. From big things to small things, I do my best when I stage manage to make sure my crew has everything they need to have a great show. In the end, it makes my job easier because I'll have a happy crew willing to do whatever is needed to have a successful show, and more often than not, it makes staffing my next show easier as they'll ask to work with me again on crew.

A Stage Manager's Survival Guide: From Callbacks to Closing

Chapter 8: Opening

Congratulations! You have made it through tech week, which likely included a preview or two! I always think that alone deserves an award. Now the adrenaline rush that is live performance can truly begin as the show is ready for opening night! Hopefully, before this night, you've had a chance to enjoy the time you spent creating this piece of art with the cast and director before sharing it with the public. Those moments are precious and worth savoring. However, we're all really in show business because we want to share our art with the world! So on with opening night!!

SURVIVAL TIP #29: SLEEP!

First things first, you just came off of a sleep-deprived tech week. While you will likely still have a long list of last minute things to do before the curtain goes up for opening, make sure to get some serious sleep! If you're not able to get a full eight hours the night before, take a good long nap the day of. If that isn't possible, make the time to relax in some way or another. Being well rested for opening has helped me for many shows. The rest allows me to call cues more clearly, think of a new solution to that set change that keeps going wrong, and to make sure I have everything I need to run a great show and enjoy opening night. A stage manager puts the cast and crew before their own needs more often than not. This is one time where you must make your health and well-being a priority. If you absolutely can't find time to catch a few Zs or rest before getting to the theatre on opening night, try to arrive at least 30 minutes before you had planned to be there. Sit in your car, in the green room, or in the booth and close your eyes for those 30 minutes. Even that can help refresh you for the night. Just get some sleep! Your cast and crew will thank you for it.

A Stage Manager's Survival Guide: From Callbacks to Closing

SURVIVAL TIP #30: Double checking.

The other important thing to do before the curtain goes up is to double-check everything. Review all the cues in your book. Do they make sense? Do you have any notes or tidbits that are needed for the cues? Do you have any remaining questions about the timing or how to call them? Although mostly I just double check that I have them all in the right place and I understand which ones go together, when sound goes first, or the lights need to wait for the set change to finish, etc. Along with the cues, double check your script in general. Are any of the pages getting a little loose and need the three-hole punch re-enforcements? In general, is your script as ready as you want it to be? Typically, I find that I have to re-enforce the last page of the script, as it's the most wobbly, but otherwise just making sure I have my script with me is the bulk of that double-check.

Bigger items to check are the checklists themselves. Are your pre-show, intermission and post-show checklists up to date? Make sure you have also printed out any extra copies needed for posting backstage or to distribute to the crew. Also, double-check that you have the most up to date shift sheets ready to distribute to the crew, and that any lists of scenes or songs posted backstage are correct and up to date. Typically, when scene changes happen doesn't tend to differentiate between the first day of tech and opening. However, the contents of the scene shift scenes will be dramatically different.

Before heading off to the theatre, it's also good to double-check your stage manager kit. Specifically for first-aid items, sewing kit items, and glow tape. I can't tell you how many times I've had an actor on opening night get stressed out because the first aid kit in the green room was out of Band-Aids, or someone found a new way to cross backstage before the show and realized glow tape was desperately needed. And don't get me started on the buttons. Even with the costumer there, when four people have a button pop, having a sewing kit and being able to pitch in helped to keep the cast and costumer calm so she could sew three of the buttons to my one. But that one she didn't have to do meant she was able to help with something else, or actually go and watch the show she had worked so hard to design.

A Stage Manager's Survival Guide: From Callbacks to Closing

More recently, I also double check that I have some form of caffeine available. My current favorite is chocolate-covered coffee beans. While typically the adrenaline rush of opening night is enough to keep me wide awake and alert, I've had a few shows where some of my cast were coming to the show after having worked a long day. That little extra bit of caffeine helps perk them up, and is something they can quickly eat in costume without risking damaging the costume or make-up. A single bean is much less likely to spill and stain than a cup of coffee! But of course, none of my cast would ever dream of eating anything once in costume, ever. Nudge, nudge. Wink wink.

SURVIVAL TIP #31: Stay calm. You got this!

With the final checklist tasks completed, the house filling up, and moments away from calling places, remind yourself of one thing: you got this! You must have confidence in your abilities and know that the magic of opening night will see you through any of the rough patches that might remain. You've rehearsed, you've tech'ed, and you are READY. So take a breath, and remain calm. Staying calm on opening night can be the biggest challenge of all as everyone is excited to see all of the hard work come to life. I can't even begin to list the amount of shows that I still had a rough page or two where I couldn't quite get the cues right, yet on opening night – tada! Like magic they worked perfectly. This holds true for crazy set changes, lightning fast costume changes, and cue lines that were never said properly before. Everything pulls together on this glorious night. So trust in yourself, after calling places but before calling the lights down, take a quick moment to take a deep breath. Close your eyes. Remove everything from your mind so you can focus only on the show. For the next few hours, nothing in the world matters outside of that theatre and that play, and you are so ready for whatever live theater will throw at you! Even if you don't think you are ready, trust me, you are. So remember that!

SURVIVAL TIP #32: Have fun, but not hangover fun.

There are so many parts of opening night that I enjoy and look forward to with each show. Almost as exhilarating of a feeling as calling that first cue is

A Stage Manager's Survival Guide: From Callbacks to Closing

calling the house ups cue at the end of the performance. The giant exhale that comes along with it because regardless of how things went, we made it through to the end! For a few shows, opening night was the first time I ran through the entire show from start to finish and in the proper order. On those nights especially, the house lights coming up means it's time to celebrate!

    I highly encourage you to enjoy that opening night. Savor the moment because every opening is unique. From the cast, the crew, the directors, the designers, the audience and the house staff, you all came together on that night to share something new with the world. However, remember that you are still the stage manager. So celebrate like a rock star, but NOT to the point that you will have a bad hangover the next day. Especially if you have a matinee the next day! Having too much fun that one night can easily cost you any future shows at that theatre company. I've been on crew for a show where the stage manager enjoyed a few too many tequila shots at the opening night party. The matinee the next day was painful for him, but worse on the crew as we couldn't rely on the stage manager to properly call the show. Fortunately, the stage manager had given us all scripts and we had a pretty good idea of when spots, lights, and sound were supposed to happen, but the show wasn't as tight as when it was called properly. This experience also taught me to include a mini hangover kit for any show that is the day after opening, or a really big cast party. Basically, I bring crackers, small Gatorade bottles, and lots of Excedrin. Because we are all human and can make this mistake. As a stage manager, I'm not there to judge, but to help make sure everyone is able to give their best performance. The hangover kit also doubles nicely as a stomach flu kit, or as one of my casts called it the "food poison recovery kit."

A Stage Manager's Survival Guide: From Callbacks to Closing

Chapter 9: The Run

Opening night is now behind you and you have the whole run out in front. Depending on the theatre, this may range from three to eight performances to four to five weekends of performances. Regardless of how many individual shows there are, it's now time to settle in and enjoy all of your hard work. The director and designers are gone and off on their next projects. The show is now in the hands of your cast, crew and you!

SURVIVAL TIP #33: Keep it fresh and consistent.

The first few performances are easy to be consistent. It's all fresh in everyone's mind. You haven't done the show in front of countless audiences. However, after that second weekend, or heck, sometimes after the third performance, the temptation to change the blocking a bit, move a cue here and there, change how the monologue is said, pause a bit more at key moments, becomes harder to resist. It is important that you remind the cast, crew and yourself, the importance of staying true to the director's vision. Every audience deserves to see the same performance audiences enjoyed on opening night.

However, there are times when making slight adjustments is helpful and necessary. For example, in *Amadeus*, Constanze had a dress that would brush up against a plate of desserts when she was lifted on the table. It was critical to the scene that she be on the table, but much less critical to have that specific tray of treats. Before removing it, I made sure to double check that the director was ok with the change. While it might be a "small change", any change is important to at least talk to the director about. It doesn't need to be a big formal conversation. A quick email or phone call is fine if you don't happen to see them in person. She was fine with the change, and the end result was that we no longer had fake food falling from a table distracting from the scene. As the stage manager, it is up to you to know when something is a

A Stage Manager's Survival Guide: From Callbacks to Closing

necessary adjustment and when it is people straying too far from the original performance.

Something else to be aware of, especially when working with younger or new to theatre casts and crew, is the prank. Occasionally the cast and crew will pull little pranks here and there as a way to have fun and keep things fresh. Be sure to communicate your expectations about pranks early in the run. Your stance should vary from cast to cast and from theatre to theatre. In general, my stance is that as long as it doesn't in any way alter what happens on stage, doesn't touch or damage the costumes, set, or props, then fine. However, if I find out about any of the pranks in advance, I will most likely remove it. For some teenage casts, I've had to be stricter as I knew they would push the limits. Such as placing fake dog poop in the drawer of the vanity for *Guys And Dolls*. The problem with that prank is that it can cause a different reaction from the actress on stage during the scene and throw off her performance. Another example that starts off innocent enough: I've been known to do hand puppet shows in the booth that only the ensemble staring out into space can see. Although when an actor told me it almost made him break character, I stopped. My intent was to help them pass the time and amuse them, but not to the extent that they ever broke character. After all at the end of the day, it is all about providing a consistent performance.

SURVIVAL TIP #34: HAVE FUN!

During the run, it is easy for a stage manager to get too serious. It's hard work making sure everything is taken care of for every show in every way possible. This is why it is important you find ways to have fun and enjoy! Often times this can be a quiet happy dance to celebrate nailing a tough cue sequence. Other times it can be joining the cast for intermission chatter, or making sure everyone is quiet on headset for your favorite line that ALWAYS makes you laugh. Speaking of headsets, it might be talking with the crew over headset and creating alternate lyrics to the songs in the show that provides you with entertainment. Whatever it is, find what works for you so that you have fun. There is a saying "happy wife, happy life." I'd say the theater version is

A Stage Manager's Survival Guide: From Callbacks to Closing

"Happy stage manager, happy show." When you are enjoying and having fun, everyone can tell and it's contagious.

It's also important to help the cast and crew continue to bond. I don't mean that you need to force them into doing trust exercises. But try having a group warm-up or just have the group come together for a quick circle and "go team" talk before the house opens. For smaller casts, this might not be needed as all five people can bond and hang out in the green room. This tip is most necessary with the large casts and crews. Make the warm-ups goofy or more practical depending on the mood. Don't feel like you have to lead them all, ask different cast or crew members to lead each night. I've found for the more intense dramatic shows, a group circle and quick chat can help focus everyone. For *Dead Man Walking*, I didn't really want everyone having a giggle fit right before the curtain goes up, but I did want everyone to come together as a group and support each other in the emotional ride that was about to happen.

Another thing to think of is making sure the cast and crew have something to do in the green room that can keep them entertained, yet quiet. Many folks will take it upon themselves to keep busy, which is fine, but this can often isolate everyone. Again, depending on the group that might be fine. Personally though, I've had the best times working on a show when we all laughed and hung out together, not separately. Having trivia cards, any variety of trivia, in the green room is a quick and easy way to bring everyone together, keep them relatively quiet, and start random conversations. Usually this works best with non-trivial pursuit cards, but even those have resulted in some conversations that make me laugh to this day. Classic multi-player video games can also be lots of fun, just make sure there is a way to have the game quiet enough that it won't be heard outside of the green room. Really it's just about helping folks find common ground and have fun together.

SURVIVAL TIP #35: Don't get comfy.

Once you have really settled into the run, typically the third week for me, is when a stage manager can fall victim to the most deadly of things, being too comfortable. The warnings, standby's and go's suddenly start being closer

A Stage Manager's Survival Guide: From Callbacks to Closing

together as folks on headset relax and start talking more. It's usually around the end of week three when my board op learns that I am the master of the "standby-go" cue, instead of "standby" followed later by "go". Not a good thing to happen. Even worse is when you get so caught up in something other than the show you forget there is supposed to be a blackout light cue at the end of a scene or musical number. Only when you here the dreaded silence on stage do you realize what happened. The best way to avoid this is to be aware of the potential, and not to let yourself fall into the comfortable trap.

    Each stage manager needs to find their own way to avoid getting too comfortable. For shows that have lots of gaps in between cues, I'll often have some Play-doh or Smart Putty to keep me occupied, yet still allow me to follow along in my script. For the shows that barely have any cues at all, I'll usually have a few quiet games on my smart phone that can help pass the time. The one thing I don't recommend is having a book. If you are the light op, great! Read all the books you want, because the stage manager will give you a warning. When you're the stage manager, there is no one else to give you a warning.

    For the shows with tons of cues and only a few little gaps here and there, I'll try to keep it fresh by watching a different ensemble member each night. Or trying to find something new in a scene I hadn't noticed before. This works wonderfully with large casts, especially when I tell the ensemble, as they'll start doing little things here and there to see if I noticed. Of course, nothing too distracting or anything that changes the director's vision of the show. Perhaps it's just the way they hold their hand when bowing in a scene, or the way they say a line, or even carry on a prop. Just as the cast works hard to keep the show fresh for the audience each night, you must work hard to keep it precise and accurate, and never take the timing of things for granted.

A Stage Manager's Survival Guide: From Callbacks to Closing

Chapter 10: Closing

No matter how amazing or stressful a show is, they all must come to an end. I've been fortunate enough to have quite a few shows that I truly wished the run would never end. Of course, there have also been one or two that couldn't end fast enough. Regardless of which category the show falls into, they all must run their course and ultimately have a closing night.

SURVIVAL TIP #36: Acknowledge the work everyone did.

It's amazing to think that only a few months before closing night, everyone was coming together for the first rehearsal. On this night, take a moment to look back and realize how much everyone contributed to get to this closing night. You should also make sure to thank and acknowledge everyone for the work they did. It doesn't matter if it's in a card, an email, a gift, or a brief speech to the cast and crew before the final curtain. Whatever is your style, do that. And it doesn't matter if they were your favorite ASM ever, or the most frustrating and insulting actor ever. EVERYONE in the show worked hard, made sacrifices. And while you might not get along with them, take the high road and acknowledge the work they did. Because I promise, every single person involved in the cast and crew worked hard. You might not have seen it, or it might not have been as hard as you hoped, but giving them credit for what they did could be what motivates them to do even more next time. As someone who has been that nearly invisible crew person, the stage managers who acknowledged my work and part in the show, small though it was, are the ones I kept coming back to work for. So remember that when you are the stage manager. Again, it doesn't need to be a grand gesture. For large casts, since I love to bake, I'll often bake a cake that can be shared with everyone (before they are in costume of course). For smaller casts and crew, I might do a little something for each individual. Also, find out which of the designers will be there. Much like a stage manager never gets flowers, the designers often don't

A Stage Manager's Survival Guide: From Callbacks to Closing

get thank you notes. Without everyone involved, the show wouldn't have been the production it was. Being known as a stage manager who isn't afraid to show gratitude and appreciation is a great way to be invited back to that theatre and get offers from other theatres, because it's all about your reputation! There is no room for arrogance and bad attitudes in theatre. Acknowledging how hard everyone else worked on the show is a great way to demonstrate that you value them and bring a positive mentality to the show.

SURVIVAL TIP #37: Enjoy not being in charge!

With the final curtain down, there is only one thing left to do, strike! Also known as tearing down the set and generally cleaning up the costumes, props and anything else from the show. The amount of work involved with this will vary greatly from show to show and theatre to theatre. For community and semi-professional theatres, you'll likely be rolling up your sleeves and helping tear down the set. For professional theatres, this is when you do a happy dance as the union crew comes in to tear down the set, although you'll likely still have some clean up tasks to do before you're done. Either way, this is when I get to say my favorite thing when working on a show, "Don't ask me, ask the tech director. He's running the strike." Because the second strike starts, your responsibilities (for the most part) are done. You aren't to blame for everything. You aren't the one who has to make sure every last thing is done. You are now one of the happy workers, right along with the cast and the crew. Typically, there will be a technical director coordinating the strike. That is the person who is in charge. Mwahahaha. Enjoy this! Make sure you work hard, and don't be afraid to nudge others to do the same, but enjoy not being the one to make all the calls. Where do the flats go? Not your decision! Where do the costumes go? Not your decision! Enjoy it while it lasts, because the second you have your next call back, you're responsible for things again. So savor this messy, dusty moment.

A Stage Manager's Survival Guide: From Callbacks to Closing

SURVIVAL TIP #38: Rest and reward

With the final show and strike complete, make sure to take some time to rest and to reward yourself for a job well done. Depending on your life, the amount of rest might be a few months, a few weeks or a day. Just make sure to give yourself a little down time to catch up on life and generally recharge your stage manager battery. If you don't, you'll start the next show exhausted and likely won't be able to give it your all. As a result, you won't be able to be the amazing stage manager you are. The show suffers, and since people notice things like this, your reputation can suffer. Granted, I had to experiment before finding the right balance of shows, so try different amounts of rest. Perhaps you take four months off from stage managing, but you work run crew on a show or two in between. Whatever works for you and your current lifestyle. Over the years I've gone from doing back-to-back shows with only a day or two off in between, to now only doing one show a year. The rest time has changed depending on what was going on in my world. Remember it is up to you to make sure you get enough rest in between shows.

As for the reward part, it's all too easy to just dive into the next project without really stopping to acknowledge what you accomplished. Stage managers don't typically receive massive amounts of public recognition, so make sure you at least take stock and pat yourself on the back for all of the time, energy and effort you put into the show. Go get a massage. Go see a movie. Or just sit and enjoy not being in charge of any actors or crew for a moment.

SURVIVAL TIP #39: Even the worst show closes, and makes the best stories

Not every show will be a ball of fun. Every now and then there is that tough one. The show might be a long one with not much for you to do, you might have an insane amount of never ending cues, there might be a diva in the cast who just won't play well with others, people might be having too much fun back stage and forget entrances, or the props became a character of their own and not in a good way. I have found those awful moments can make for the most hysterical stories. Perhaps it wasn't the entire run that was painful,

A Stage Manager's Survival Guide: From Callbacks to Closing

just an odd moment or two. Either way, it's important to be able to laugh at the experience and learn from it.

Just know that this too shall pass, and when chatting in post-show gatherings for future shows, you'll have GREAT fodder for "you wouldn't believe what happened" stories. Here are some of my personal favorites, take a guess at how many directly relate to a specific tip.

- An actor slept through his curtain call.
- There was the heaviest and most complicated (but gorgeous) opera set that required excessive drills for each change.
- That damn ironing board (a prop that was *supposed* to start the top of the show on stage).
- A set piece that fell on a crew member during the scene change resulting in her getting stitches.
- The plant. Always that awful big smelly Audrey II plant.
- Futuristic space beer, which was ultimately saved by Jell-O.
- When the light board computer decided to reboot in the middle of a set change (so the lights were dim and stayed on until the board decided it was done rebooting and I could take the next cue).

The best one I've ever heard didn't actually happen to me, but to a fellow stage manager. At the start of the second act, after intermission, the house lights went out and the stage lights went up. The actor walked on stage. Stopped. Looked up at the booth and said something to the effect of, "Sorry. We need to start over, I need to use the restroom."

I always love hearing and sharing these stories with fellow stage managers and theatre folks in general. If anything, I've always found it reassuring to know the crazy and stressful stuff doesn't just happen to me, but to all of us. No matter how experienced you are, you never know what new story and laugh is lurking around the corner.

A Stage Manager's Survival Guide: From Callbacks to Closing

SURVIVAL TIP #40: Remember there is always something new to learn

My last tip is one that, as the years go by, is the easiest to forget. Whether it's your first show or your 60th, there is always something new to learn. Be sure to apply your previous learnings to ever show as best you can, and look forward to what new tip or trick you'll discover next.

When you think you know it all, you're wrong and should talk to a fellow stage manager. Since no two people are the same, no two shows will ever be the same. There is always some new technology out there, some new way to approach a rehearsal, a new way to communicate to the staff, etc. Even on shows that run smoothly, take a look back to see what made it smooth so you'll be able to keep things smooth for your next show.

One of my favorite ways to learn new things is to assistant stage manager for someone. Preferably a stage manager you admire, but honestly you can learn plenty from working with the not-so-great ones as well. Another method is to chat with your recent director, crew and cast to find out how they thought things went. I'm personally someone who learns best by observing and doing, so I prefer the ASM route. Figure out how you learn best though. There are tons of stage manager blogs and websites out there. Read through some to see what other stage managers are talking about and how their solving things. About 10 years ago, I was part of a stage manager forum and found it very helpful to be able to ask my peers a specific question and get their advice. Just make an ongoing effort to keep learning. If you're able to do that, and keep in mind the other 39 tips, you are likely to have many wonderful shows where you'll be referred to as "the amazing stage manager" by all involved.

By: Michelle Marko, copyright 2015

A Stage Manager's Survival Guide: From Callbacks to Closing

Acknowledgements

For the book:

    I would like to acknowledge City Lights Theater Company for giving me the push and reason to actually write this book, especially Lisa Mallette and Ron Gasparinetti, who late one night after rehearsal said, "You should write a book!" Just like a show, it took a village to make this book happen. I couldn't have done it without my friends who kindly helped with editing; April Rauer, Marin Page and Chris McCrellis-Mitchell. A special thank you to Evelyn Huynh for her patience in taking my headshot. Also to the many actors, crew, designers, and friends who have inspired me and gave me great stories to share.

My inspiration:

    I wanted to take a moment to acknowledge a few people and shows. In my acknowledgements above I mention the folks who have helped with this book. However, it is important to me that I also take a moment to mention the specific shows and a few key people who have spurred my theatre career on and made me the stage manager I am today.

    Starting with one amazing woman. Without her, none of the last countless years of theatre would have happened for me. I am referring to the one-and- only Shareen Miriam who was my high school drama teacher and the woman who introduced me to the backstage world. Right along with her was another teacher from another high school that I had the honor of working with, Tim Shannon. He showed me that being in tech was a wonderful choice people made because they loved it, not because they sucked at acting. While I've always loved theatre, those two people started me on my path to stage management and I am forever grateful. I also owe a big thank you to my mom, who forced 13-year-old me to go to an improv workshop. That was where I not only made lifelong friends and mentors (and crew members), but also learned how to fail big and not just be okay with it, but be able to laugh at it. As a stage manager, and in life, that skill has been incredibly handy.

    Now for the shows that stand out to me as some of the most special

A Stage Manager's Survival Guide: From Callbacks to Closing

and amazing ones. *Midsummer Night's Dream*: both the production in high school which was my first time ever backstage, and the post-college production that was my first outdoor show. *Lion In The Streets*: the first full production I stage managed in college. An amazing play and also was when I was able to work with a director who had been a professional stage manager. *Baltimore Waltz*: my last full college production (I was the ASM). *Chicago*: my favorite college musical and that UCSB version is still my favorite that I've seen (beating out Broadway and the West End). *Brigadoon*: my favorite post-college musical where I had a bit too much fun with my good friend who was the spot op playing spotlight tag during a particular number. *The Dining Room*: a wonderful cast and director. I still don't look at Cool Whip or potato flakes the same. *On The Verge:* an amazing cast and a show where I learned to stand up for myself and the management learned how protective I am of my cast. *Complete Works of Shakespeare Abridged*: inflatable Godzilla, I still laugh at the photos, this was also the first show I worked on, as crew, at a theatre that has long since become my second home. *Carmen*: the first opera I worked on, and where I realized how much I love opera. *Sylvia*: not only was the cast fantastic, but as an animal lover, the play truly touched me. *Dead Man Walking* and *Compleat Female Stage Beauty*: my director, cast and crew were better than the movies! I'm biased, but still right. You just can't beat our golden palm fronds, "sparkle bums", bawdy dance, or the intense emotions of the electrocution scene. This was also when I learned how wonderful it is to be in tune with your director. *Christmas Shorts*: this was the cast that caused me to call my wonderful actors "my angels", we became a family that lived on after the show and created many great memories. And I won't say "last" because this show is the one that recharged my battery, so I'll say most recently, *Amadeus* will close out this list as it was a once-in-a-lifetime show where we created an award winning piece of work that I was extremely honored to have been a part of.

About the author

Michelle has spent her life in local theatre, starting with kindergarten plays where she was the second mouse or the sister or such. At the age of 15 she realized she wasn't passionate about being ON stage. It was then that she signed up for props crew, was made the props manager and transitioned from onstage to backstage.

She has spent over 20 years as a stage manager for various colleges, community, local professional and semi-professional theatres. In that time she has gone from knowing everything (ah the joy that is being 18) to realizing how much she had to learn (the joy that is being over 21). She received her under graduate degree in Technical Theatre with an emphasis on stage management from the University of California, Santa Barbara.

These days she describes herself as an experienced stage manager who knows enough to be dangerous, but firmly believes there is always more to learn. She gives her heart and soul to every production, doing everything within her power to make sure each show is the best it can possibly be for the audience, while having as much fun as possible along the way.

The epiphany that she didn't actually know it all at 18 was the inspiration for this book. If only someone had shared with her back then what she knows now, she could have avoided many tough lessons learned, embarrassing moments and unnecessary stress. Of course, she wouldn't trade any of the hilarity and "you did what?!" moments for the world, those she highly encourages everyone to go and experience!

Made in the USA
San Bernardino, CA
12 November 2017